UPDATED

KOS

TRAVEL GUIDE

2023 | 2024

Kos Explorer's Guide Book: A Journey Through Island Paradise

PAT Z. WESTFIELD

TABLE OF CONTENTS

CHAPTER FIVE 114

CHAPTER SIX 134

CHAPTER SEVEN 152

CHAPTER EIGHT 168

CHAPTER NINE 182

IMPORTANT NOTICE TO TRAVELERS

"THIS TRAVEL GUIDE DOES NOT CONTAIN IMAGES BECAUSE EVERY LOCATION IN HERE AS BEEN THOUGHTFULLY AND SCENICALLY DESCRIBED, MOREOVER

THE MOST BREATHTAKING IMAGES WILL BE THE ONES PAINTED BY YOUR VERY OWN EYES AS YOU VENTURE INTO A WORLD DIFFERENT FROM WHAT YOU ARE USED TO."

Pat Z. Westfield

CHAPTER ONE

WELCOME TO KOS

Welcome to the enchanting island of Kos, a true jewel in the heart of the Aegean Sea. Nestled among the Dodecanese islands of Greece, Kos is a destination that beckons travelers from across the globe with its captivating blend of history, natural beauty, and vibrant culture. This comprehensive guide is your key to unlocking the treasures of this Greek paradise, providing you with all the essential information and guidance you need to make your visit to Kos an unforgettable experience.

Kos is a place where history comes to life beneath the radiant Mediterranean sun. It's an island where you can stroll through ancient ruins, soak in the crystal-clear waters of pristine beaches, and savor the flavors of authentic Greek cuisine. It doesn't matter if you're a history enthusiast, a nature lover, an adventure seeker, or simply looking for a serene escape, Kos has something special to offer you

What Makes Kos Stand-out

Kos is not just another Greek island; it's a destination that stands out for a myriad of reasons, each contributing to its unique charm and allure. As you prepare to embark on your journey to this enchanting Aegean paradise, let's delve into what makes Kos truly exceptional

1. Ancient History and Culture

Kos holds the distinguished honor of being the birthplace of Hippocrates, the father of modern medicine. Visitors can explore the ancient Asklepion, an archaeological site where Hippocrates once practiced and taught his healing arts. The legacy of this great physician permeates the island, making it a haven for those interested in medical history and ancient healing practices.

Archaeological Marvels: The island is sprinkled with remnants of its illustrious past. Explore the Agora, ancient temples, Roman villas, and medieval castles that tell stories of empires and civilizations that have left their mark on Kos over the centuries.

2. Natural Beauty

Beaches for Every Taste: Kos boasts a diverse range of beaches, from bustling and vibrant to secluded and serene. Whether you seek the lively atmosphere of Kardamena Beach, the golden sands of Tigaki, or the tranquil coves of Agios Stefanos, there's a beach to suit your mood.

Lush Landscapes: Beyond the shoreline, Kos reveals a world of natural wonders. Verdant valleys, rolling hills, and towering mountains offer a stunning backdrop for exploration. Don't miss the opportunity to hike in the Zia Natural Park, where you can witness breathtaking sunsets and panoramic views.

Thermal Springs: Kos is known for its therapeutic thermal springs, making it a destination for wellness seekers. Enjoy a rejuvenating soak in natural hot springs like Agios Fokas or Psalidi, believed to have healing properties.

3. Warm Hospitality

Friendly Locals: The people of Kos are known for their warm and welcoming nature. You'll quickly feel like a part of the community as you interact with locals who are eager to share their culture and traditions.

Traditional Festivals: Immerse yourself in the island's culture by participating in traditional festivals and celebrations. Witness colorful processions, dance to Greek music, and savor local delicacies during events like the "Kos Wine Festival" and religious celebrations.

4. Culinary Delights

Greek Gastronomy: Greek cuisine is renowned worldwide, and Kos offers an array of delectable dishes. Savor classic Greek flavors like moussaka, souvlaki, and tzatziki, along with locally sourced seafood and farm-fresh produce.

Visit charming tavernas and waterfront restaurants to indulge in mouthwatering seafood delicacies, accompanied by the island's signature drink, ouzo.

Vineyards and Olive Groves: Discover the island's rich agricultural heritage by visiting vineyards and olive groves. Taste locally produced wines and olive oils, which are among the finest in Greece.

5. Relaxed Atmosphere

While Kos offers plenty of activities and attractions, it maintains a laid-back, peaceful atmosphere. It's the perfect place to unwind, relax, and escape the hustle and bustle of everyday life.

Island-Hopping Opportunities: Positioned among the Dodecanese islands, Kos serves as an excellent base for exploring neighboring islands like Rhodes, Patmos, and Kalymnos, adding another layer of versatility to your trip.

In conclusion, Kos stands out as a multifaceted destination that seamlessly blends its rich historical heritage with breathtaking natural beauty, warm hospitality, delectable cuisine, and an inviting atmosphere.

How to use this guidebook

To make the most of your journey through Kos, it's important to understand how this guide is organized. We've carefully structured it to provide you with a comprehensive overview of the island, including practical information, insider tips, and inspiring recommendations. Each chapter and subchapter has been designed to help you navigate through the different facets of Kos, ensuring that you have all the tools and knowledge you need for an extraordinary adventure.

If you're planning a week-long getaway, an extended vacation, or just a quick escape to paradise, this guide is your trusted companion for discovering the wonders of Kos. Let's embark on this incredible journey together, starting with an exploration of the island's geography, climate, and rich history in the next section. Welcome to Kos!

Brief History and Overview of Kos

Kos, the captivating Greek island nestled in the Aegean Sea, boasts a history that stretches back thousands of years. Its story begins in the mists of prehistory, with the first evidence of human settlement dating to around 3,500 BC. These early inhabitants left behind archaeological traces in locations like Asclepius, a prehistoric settlement, which offer a glimpse into the island's ancient past.

The Influence of Antiquity

However, it was during the Classical period that Kos truly began to shine on the world stage. Around 460 BC, the island gained worldwide renown as the birthplace of Hippocrates, the father of modern medicine. Here, he founded the famed Asclepion, an ancient healing center that doubled as a medical school. The teachings of Hippocrates laid the foundations for modern medical practices and ethics, and the Hippocratic Oath, a pledge to uphold medical ethics, is still taken by physicians today.

During antiquity, Kos was a coveted prize for various empires and city-states. It experienced Persian rule, followed by Athenian control, and eventually became a part of the Ptolemaic dynasty of Egypt. This diverse influence resulted in a thriving economy and a rich cultural tapestry. Notable ruins from this era include the Asklepion, a healing center adorned with grand temples and monuments.

Roman and Byzantine Eras

With the rise of the Roman Empire, Kos continued to prosper. It became a Roman province in 129 BC and saw the construction of impressive structures like the Roman Odeon, a small theater that hosted various performances and events. This era brought further development to the island's infrastructure.

As the Roman Empire declined, Kos transitioned into the Byzantine era. During this time, it evolved into a center of Christianity. Numerous churches and monasteries were built, showcasing Byzantine architectural styles and religious devotion. The remnants of these religious edifices are still visible today, adding depth to Kos's historical heritage.

Medieval and Ottoman Rule

Kos's history is marked by the medieval period, which saw a succession of rulers. The Knights of St. John and the Venetians both held sway over the island at different times. During these years, the island's cultural identity continued to evolve, incorporating elements from various Mediterranean cultures. This era left a mark on the island's cuisine, architecture, and traditions, resulting in the unique blend of Greek and Turkish influences seen today.

In 1523, Kos fell under Ottoman rule, which would endure for nearly four centuries. This period significantly shaped the island's identity, as it became a bridge between East and West. The Ottoman influence is evident in the island's architecture, cuisine, and even its customs. Visitors can still witness remnants of this era in the charming narrow streets and historic buildings of Kos Town.

Modern Times

Kos's modern history is marked by several notable events. In 1912, during the Greco-Turkish War, the island was liberated from Ottoman rule, joining the newly independent Greece. In the decades that followed, Kos experienced various changes in sovereignty, including brief occupations by the Italians and Germans during World War II.

Since Greece's independence, Kos has grown into a vibrant tourist destination, welcoming travelers from around the globe. Its pristine beaches, clear blue waters, and bustling nightlife have made it a top choice for those seeking both relaxation and adventure. Meanwhile, its ancient ruins, archaeological sites, and rich cultural traditions continue to beckon history enthusiasts and culture seekers.

Overview

In contemporary times, Kos remains a hub of tourism, offering a harmonious blend of history, culture, and natural beauty. With a Mediterranean climate that provides warm, sun-soaked summers and mild winters, the island is a year-round destination. The warmth and hospitality of the local residents, the tantalizing Greek cuisine, and the enduring historical legacy all combine to create an unforgettable experience for every visitor.

As you explore Kos, you'll find yourself in a place where history seamlessly mingles with the stunning landscapes—a destination that captures the very essence of Greece's timeless charm. Whether you're lounging on its pristine beaches, marveling at ancient ruins, or savoring local delicacies, Kos promises an enriching and unforgettable journey through time.

Geography and Location

Kos, an island of captivating beauty and historical significance, is situated in the southeastern part of the Aegean Sea, making it an ideal destination for those seeking both relaxation and exploration. Let's dive deeper into the island's geography and location to provide a comprehensive understanding of what makes Kos so unique.

Island Geography

Kos boasts a diverse and mesmerizing topography, providing an array of landscapes that cater to a wide range of interests and activities.

- **Coastlines**: The island's coastline stretches for more than 100 kilometers, offering a mix of sandy, pebbly, and even some rocky beaches. From the lively and organized beaches near Kos Town to the tranquil and untouched coves in remote areas, Kos has something for every beachgoer. The crystal-clear waters of the Aegean Sea are perfect for swimming, snorkeling, and water sports.

- **Fertile Plains**: The heart of the island is covered by fertile plains, making it an agricultural haven. These plains are adorned with vineyards, olive groves, and orchards. They not only contribute to the island's culinary delights but also provide an alluring landscape of lush greenery.

- **Mountainous Terrain**: In the southwest, the island's terrain becomes mountainous, with Mount Dikeos being the highest peak. This region is a paradise for nature lovers and hikers, offering stunning panoramic views of the island and the sea. Numerous hiking trails wind through these mountains, leading to ancient ruins, picturesque villages, and hidden chapels.

Strategic Location

Kos's strategic location in the Aegean Sea has played a pivotal role in its history and continued significance as a travel destination.

- **Proximity to Turkey**: Kos is just a short ferry ride away from the Turkish coast. This proximity to

Turkey has had a profound influence on the island's culture and cuisine. It's not uncommon for visitors to take a day trip to Bodrum, a popular Turkish resort town, to experience the cross-cultural dynamics of the region.

- **Nearby Islands**: Kos is surrounded by other captivating islands in the Dodecanese archipelago. Nisyros, known for its active volcano, and Kalymnos, famous for rock climbing, are just a couple of hours away by ferry. These islands offer unique experiences, from exploring volcanic craters to embarking on adrenaline-pumping adventures.

Weather and Climate

Understanding the weather and climate of Kos is pivotal for planning your visit to this beautiful Greek island. Located in the southeastern part of the Aegean Sea, Kos boasts a Mediterranean climate that significantly influences the island's appeal throughout the year.

Understanding the Mediterranean Climate

Kos Island, like many other Mediterranean destinations, is influenced by a high-pressure weather system, characterized by the following key elements:

Warm, Dry Summers (June to September)

Kos Island's summer, which typically spans from June to September, is marked by its quintessential Mediterranean character. During this period, the island becomes a haven for sunseekers and outdoor enthusiasts. The days are bathed in abundant sunshine, and clear blue skies create a striking backdrop. Average temperatures during these months range from a comfortable 25°C to a scorching 35°C (77°F to 95°F). This season is all about embracing the great outdoors, whether you're relaxing on the island's beautiful beaches, indulging in thrilling watersports, or taking part in lively summer festivals. The long, balmy evenings are perfect for enjoying the island's vibrant nightlife and open-air dining.

Mild, Tranquil Autumns (October to November)

As summer gradually yields to autumn, Kos takes on a different ambiance. The temperatures become milder, making daytime exploration more comfortable. Evenings are cooler but still pleasant, making it ideal for leisurely strolls. Though there may be occasional rainfall during these months, it is generally not excessive. Autumn is a delightful time for travelers who want to explore the island's historical and cultural heritage without the sweltering heat of summer. It's a time when the island's natural beauty is tinged with the golden hues of fall.

Mild Winters (December to February)

Winters on Kos are notably mild compared to many other European destinations. The average temperatures in this season range between 8°C and 15°C (46°F to 59°F). While you may encounter some rainfall, it's less frequent than in many other Mediterranean regions. Winter is the quietest season for tourism, making it a time for contemplation and relaxation. It's a period when you can immerse yourself in the local culture, dine in cozy tavernas, and appreciate the island's natural beauty without the bustling crowds. The island takes on a more tranquil and authentic character during this time, making it ideal for travelers seeking a quieter, immersive experience.

Reviving Springs (March to May)

Spring in Kos is a time of rebirth and renewal. From March to May, the island undergoes a remarkable transformation as temperatures gradually rise. The natural world comes to life with a kaleidoscope of blossoming flowers and lush greenery. Springtime offers mild and pleasant weather, making it an ideal season for outdoor activities. Hiking and biking become particularly enjoyable during this period, and it's a wonderful time for exploring the island's cultural and historical sites at a leisurely pace. The island is less crowded than in summer, allowing for a deeper connection with its natural and cultural offerings.

Best Time to Visit

Planning the perfect trip to Kos depends not only on understanding the island's Mediterranean climate but also on selecting the best time to visit based on your preferences. Each season on this Greek island offers distinct experiences, making it essential to choose the timing that aligns with your travel goals.

Summer (June to September):

- **Pros**: Summer is undeniably the most popular season for tourists on Kos. During this time, the island comes alive with a bustling, vibrant atmosphere. The sun shines abundantly, the clear blue skies stretch as far as the eye can see, and temperatures range from 25°C to 35°C (77°F to 95°F). It's the epitome of a classic beach holiday, ideal for sunbathing, swimming, and partaking in a variety of water sports.

- **Activities**: Enjoy the lively beach scene, explore the island's nightlife, and immerse yourself in the energetic outdoor ambiance.

2. Spring (March to May):

- **Pros**: Spring is a charming season in Kos, offering a delightful transition from the cooler months. The island is adorned with a tapestry of blooming flowers, and the weather is mild, with temperatures becoming increasingly comfortable. This is the perfect time for those who prefer fewer crowds, outdoor adventures, and a more relaxed exploration of the island.

- **Activities**: Explore historical sites, embark on hiking and biking expeditions, and savor the island's culture.

3. Autumn (October to November):

- **Pros**: Autumn extends the milder temperatures of summer into October, providing a serene ambiance for those who wish to extend their beach time. As the season progresses, evenings grow cooler and occasional rain showers arrive. This period is perfect for travelers who want to explore the island's historical and cultural sites at a slower pace and revel in its natural beauty.

- **Activities**: Visit historical treasures, discover the island's picturesque countryside, and enjoy a quieter beach experience.

4. Winter (December to February):

- **Pros**: While winter is the quietest season on Kos, it offers a unique perspective of the island. The mild temperatures, ranging from 8°C to 15°C (46°F to 59°F), provide a more contemplative experience. Fewer tourists mean you can delve deeper into the local culture and enjoy the island's natural beauty without the bustling crowds.

- **Activities**: Visit cultural sites without the crowds, engage in quiet contemplation, and explore the island's historical and culinary offerings.

In summary, the best time to visit Kos ultimately depends on your travel style and your goals for the trip.

Essential Things to Pack On Your Trip

Preparing for your journey to Kos is an essential part of ensuring a comfortable and enjoyable trip. Knowing what to pack can make a significant difference in your travel experience. In this chapter, we'll guide you through the essential items to include in your packing list, ensuring you're well-prepared for your adventure.

Clothing and Footwear

- **Light, Breathable Clothing**: Kos has a Mediterranean climate with warm summers. Pack lightweight, breathable fabrics like cotton and linen to stay comfortable during the day.
- **Swimwear**: Don't forget your swimsuit, as you'll be spending time at the beach.
- **Sunglasses and Sun Hat**: Protect yourself from the Mediterranean sun.
- **Comfortable Walking Shoes**: You'll be exploring historical sites and natural wonders, so comfortable footwear is a must.
- **Evening Attire**: For those planning on enjoying the island's nightlife, include some stylish evening wear.

Travel Documents and Money

- **Passport and Visa**: Ensure your passport is valid for at least six months beyond your planned departure date.
- **Travel Insurance**: It's always a good idea to have travel insurance for emergencies.
- **Photocopies and Digital Copies**: Make copies of important documents and store them digitally.

- **Local Currency**: Bring some cash for small expenses, and don't forget your credit/debit cards.
- **Travel Adapter**: Greece uses the Europlug (Type C) power outlets, so bring a suitable adapter.

Health and Personal Care

- **Prescription Medications**: If you have any essential medications, be sure to pack an adequate supply.
- **First-Aid Kit**: Include basics like band-aids, pain relievers, and any personal medical supplies you might need.
- **Sunscreen and Bug Spray**: Protect your skin from the sun and insects.
- **Toiletries**: Pack your essentials, but remember you can purchase most toiletries locally if needed.

Electronics and Accessories

- **Mobile Phone and Charger**: Stay connected and consider getting a local SIM card for data.

- **Camera and Accessories**: Capture the stunning landscapes and memorable moments.
- **Power Bank**: Keep your devices charged, especially if you're out and about all day.

Travel Gear

- **Backpack or Daypack**: Ideal for carrying your daily essentials while exploring.
- **Travel Locks**: Keep your belongings secure, especially in crowded areas.
- **Reusable Water Bottle**: Save money and reduce plastic waste by refilling your own bottle.

Entertainment and Miscellaneous

- **Books, Magazines, or E-Readers**: Something to keep you entertained during downtime.
- **Language Guidebook**: A helpful tool to communicate with locals.
- **Travel Pillow and Eye Mask**: Ensure a good night's sleep during your journey.
- **Travel Umbrella**: Just in case you encounter a sudden rain shower.

By following these packing tips and knowing what to include and what to leave behind, you'll be well-prepared for your journey to Kos. Efficient packing ensures that you have the flexibility to explore, enjoy, and make the most of your time on this enchanting Greek island.

Visa and Entry Requirement

Ensuring that you meet the entry regulations and visa requirements when planning your journey to Kos is a fundamental step in guaranteeing a smooth, enjoyable trip to this captivating Greek island. In this section, we will delve deeper into the crucial entry regulations and visa essentials that every traveler should be well-informed about before embarking on their adventure to Kos.

Visa-Free Travel

One of the most significant conveniences for many travelers is that Greece, which includes the beloved island of Kos, is a proud member of the Schengen Area. This arrangement allows citizens of numerous countries, encompassing the United States, Canada, Australia, and most European nations, to enter Greece and Kos for short-term stays without the necessity of obtaining a visa beforehand. Typically, tourists from these countries can relish an uninterrupted stay for up to 90 days within a

180-day period. This liberal visa policy paves the way for a hassle-free and flexible visit to Kos.

Passport Validity

Prior to your departure, it's paramount to confirm that your passport aligns with certain stipulations:

- **Valid Passport**: Your passport must possess a validity of at least three months beyond your intended date of departure from the Schengen Area. Hence, it is prudent to review your passport's expiration date well in advance of your trip to avoid any unwelcome surprises upon arrival.

- **Blank Visa Pages**: As customs and immigration authorities may require space for entry and exit stamps, you must ensure that your passport has an adequate number of blank pages. This preparatory step is crucial to guarantee a hassle-free entry and exit process.

Visa-Exempt Countries

While the majority of travelers are fortunate to relish visa-free access to Greece and Kos, some exceptions exist. Travelers originating from countries outside the Schengen Area should take the initiative to validate their specific visa prerequisites by consulting the Greek embassies or consulates in their home countries before setting off on their journey.

Visa-on-Arrival and Visa Extensions

Greece extends the courtesy of visa-on-arrival to citizens of certain nationalities. If uncertainty looms regarding your visa status, it is highly advisable to engage with the Greek Ministry of Foreign Affairs or the Greek Embassy in your country of residence before embarking on your journey.

For those contemplating extended stays beyond the permitted 90-day period or individuals pursuing non-tourist activities such as work, study, or long-term residence, the onus is on them to diligently follow the requisite procedures for securing the appropriate visa well in advance of their departure.

Important Documents

As you embark on your journey to Kos, it is imperative to possess and carry the following essential documents:

- **Valid Passport**: Ensure your passport adheres to the passport validity requirements delineated above.

- **Return Ticket**: Immigration authorities may request evidence of your intention to exit the country within the specified time frame. Possessing a return ticket is a prudent step in this regard.

- **Travel Insurance**: While not mandated, travel insurance can be invaluable in the event of unforeseen situations. It provides peace of mind by covering medical emergencies, trip cancellations, and lost belongings.

- **Accommodation Details**: You might be required to furnish information about your place of stay while in Greece. Having this information readily available streamlines your entry process.

- **Sufficient Funds**: Being able to demonstrate access to financial resources is a crucial aspect of the entry process. This assures authorities that you can adequately cover your expenses while in Greece.

In conclusion, understanding the visa and entry requirements for Kos is pivotal in ensuring a seamless, trouble-free trip. It is prudent to proactively engage with your local Greek embassy or consulate well in advance of your planned travel date. Being well-prepared in this regard is your ticket to fully savoring the mesmerizing beauty and cultural riches that Kos has to offer, free from the inconveniences of entry-related hurdles.

CHAPTER TWO

GETTING TO AND AROUND KOS

Your journey to the enchanting island of Kos is the beginning of an unforgettable adventure. In this chapter, we'll provide you with comprehensive information on transportation to and around Kos, whether you're coming from Greece or abroad.

By Air

Kos International Airport

Kos Island International Airport, known as "Hippocrates" (IATA: KGS), serves as the primary entry point to the island. Situated conveniently in the village of Antimachia, it's approximately 24 kilometers (15 miles) from Kos Town.

Flights to Kos

The airport is well-connected with a variety of international and domestic flights. Travelers can easily access Kos from major European cities, and seasonal charter flights further enhance its accessibility.

Airport Facilities

Kos Airport boasts a range of services and amenities to make your arrival and departure convenient. These include shops, dining options, car rental services, and currency exchange facilities.

Transport to Your Destination

Upon landing at Kos Airport, you have several transportation options to reach your destination on the island. These include taxis, airport shuttles, and rental cars. These modes of transport ensure a smooth transition from your flight to the beautiful landscapes and attractions of Kos.

By Sea

Arriving via Ferries and Passenger Ships

Kos offers a maritime gateway that allows visitors to arrive by sea, providing a picturesque and memorable entry to the island. Here's a closer look at this mode of transportation:

- **Kos Port:** Serving as the principal maritime entrance, Kos Port is a bustling hub with connections to various Greek islands and even neighboring Turkey. It stands as the preferred arrival point for many travelers.

- **Kardamena Port:** In addition to the main port in Kos Town, the coastal town of Kardamena boasts its own port. While smaller in scale, it offers ferry connections and is a gateway for those staying in that part of the island.

- **Crossing from Turkey:** For travelers journeying from Bodrum, Turkey, a short ferry ride connects Bodrum to Kos. Remember to check visa requirements and ferry schedules, especially if you're planning a day trip to the neighboring country.

- **Ferry Operators:** Multiple ferry companies facilitate routes to and from Kos. Blue Star Ferries, Dodekanisos Seaways, and Turkish ferry operators handle connections to Bodrum and other nearby destinations.

The sea route to Kos not only provides efficient transportation but also offers a delightful approach, allowing you to witness the island's beauty gradually unfolding as you draw near.

Getting Around Kos

When you arrive in Kos, you'll be eager to explore all the treasures this island has to offer. Getting around Kos is a breeze, with various transportation options to suit your preferences and travel style. In this chapter, we'll guide you through the different ways to navigate the island, ensuring you can make the most of your time here.

Transportation Options

Here are the transportation options in Kos:

Renting a Car

Renting a car is a popular choice for many travelers visiting Kos, and for good reason. It offers the freedom and flexibility to explore the island at your own pace, access remote areas, and discover hidden gems that may not be easily accessible by public transportation. Here's a comprehensive guide to renting a car on the island:

Why Rent a Car?

- **Flexibility**: With a rented car, you have the freedom to create your own itinerary, explore off-the-beaten-path locations, and change your plans on a whim.

- **Convenience**: It's convenient, especially if you have a lot of luggage or if you're traveling with family. You can easily transport your belongings and stop wherever you like.

- **Time-Saving**: Renting a car can save you time, as you won't have to wait for public transportation schedules or adhere to tour group itineraries.

Renting a Car: Step by Step

1. **Booking**: Start by researching car rental agencies in Kos. Most international agencies like Hertz, Avis, and Europcar have offices on the island. Local agencies may offer competitive rates as well. You can book online in advance or visit their offices upon arrival.

2. **Driver's License**: Ensure you have a valid driver's license from your home country. Most rental agencies require drivers to be at least 21 years old, though some may have a minimum age of 23 or 25. Check the specific requirements of the rental agency you choose.

3. **Insurance**: Discuss insurance options with the rental agency. Basic insurance is usually included, but you can opt for additional coverage for extra peace of mind.

4. **Vehicle Choice**: Select a vehicle that suits your needs and group size. Compact cars are suitable for couples or solo travelers, while larger vehicles like SUVs or minivans are ideal for families or groups.

5. **Pick-up and Drop-off**: Determine where you'll pick up and drop off the car. Many agencies have offices at Kos Airport, making it convenient for

arriving travelers. You can often drop off the car at a different location if needed.

6. **Road Rules**: Familiarize yourself with Greek road rules, such as driving on the right side of the road and obeying speed limits. Road signs are in Greek and international symbols.

7. **Fuel**: Gasoline (petrol) is widely available on the island. Remember to check the fuel policy with the rental agency, as it may differ from one company to another.

8. **Parking**: Parking in Kos Town can be challenging, but there are numerous parking lots and street-side parking spots. In smaller towns and villages, parking is generally more straightforward.

9. **Exploring**: Kos offers a plethora of exciting destinations to explore by car, including historical sites like Asklepion, beautiful beaches, charming villages, and scenic mountain roads. Be prepared for the occasional narrow or winding road, especially in the mountainous areas.

10. **Return**: Return the car as per your agreement with the rental agency. Make sure to refill the tank to the level required by the agency to avoid additional charges.

Tips and Considerations

- **Book in Advance**: Especially during peak tourist season, it's a good idea to reserve your car ahead of time to secure the vehicle type you want.

- **Inspect the Car**: Before driving off, carefully inspect the vehicle for any existing damage and document it. This helps avoid disputes over damages upon returning the car.

- **GPS or Maps**: Consider renting a GPS or using a navigation app on your phone to help you find your way around the island.

- **Driving Safely**: Drive cautiously, especially on narrow and winding roads. Greek drivers can be assertive, so stay alert and patient.

Renting Scooters and ATVs

Exploring Kos on a scooter or an all-terrain vehicle (ATV) offers a thrilling and adventurous way to experience the island's natural beauty and historical wonders.

Renting a scooter or ATV is a popular choice for those seeking an exciting and more hands-on way to explore Kos. Here's what you need to know:

1. **Age and License Requirements**

- To rent a scooter, you usually need to be at least 18 years old, while for an ATV, the minimum age requirement might be 21.

- A valid driver's license is typically required. An international driver's permit is recommended for non-EU visitors.

2. Rental Agencies

- Kos has numerous rental agencies that offer scooters and ATVs for hire. You'll find them in popular tourist areas, at the airport, and in the main town. Websites like TripAdvisor or travel forums are valuable resources. Many travelers share their experiences and recommendations for rental companies on these platforms.

- Shop around for the best rental rates and be sure to inspect the vehicle before accepting it to note any pre-existing damage.

3. Safety Gear

- Helmets are mandatory for both scooter and ATV riders. Ensure the rental agency provides you with a good-quality helmet.

- Other safety gear like gloves and protective clothing is advisable, especially if you plan to venture off-road.

4. Riding Rules and Regulations

- Follow local traffic laws and speed limits. Remember that traffic in Greece drives on the right side of the road.

- Respect off-limits areas, such as archaeological sites and nature reserves.

Benefits of Scooters and ATVs

Riding a scooter or ATV on Kos offers several advantages:

Flexibility: Scooters and ATVs can navigate through narrow streets and congested areas, allowing you to reach destinations that may be challenging with a larger vehicle.

Scenic Routes: These vehicles provide a unique perspective of the island's landscapes. Enjoy the wind in your hair as you ride along coastal roads and through picturesque villages.

Adventure: Off-roading is an option with ATVs, offering an adventurous way to explore Kos's rugged terrain and hidden gems.

Parking: Scooters and ATVs are easy to park, making it simple to stop and explore wherever you like.

Safety Considerations

While scooters and ATVs offer an exciting way to explore, safety should always be a priority:

Training: If you're not experienced in riding scooters or ATVs, consider taking a short lesson or practicing in a safe area before hitting the road.

Road Conditions: Some roads on Kos may be in less-than-ideal conditions, so drive cautiously and be prepared for unexpected obstacles.

Weather: Be mindful of the weather, especially on windy or rainy days, as it can affect your riding experience.

Traffic: Be aware of other drivers, especially during the tourist season when roads can become congested.

Taxis

Taxis are a convenient and widely available mode of transportation on the island of Kos. Whether you need a quick ride to your hotel, want to explore a specific destination, or simply prefer the comfort of a private ride, taxis are at your service. In this section, we'll provide you with all the essential information you need to make the most of the taxi services in Kos.

Benefits of Using Taxis:

- **Convenience:** Taxis are available at the airport, ferry terminals, major hotels, and popular tourist areas, making it easy to find a ride when you need one.

- **Comfort:** Taxis are air-conditioned, providing relief from the Greek sun. Most drivers are polite and helpful, making your journey pleasant and comfortable.

- **Quick and Direct:** Taxis offer a direct route to your destination, ensuring you don't waste time on unnecessary stops or detours.

Fares and Pricing:

- **Pricing Structure:** Taxis in Kos operate on a meter system. However, it's advisable to clarify the fare with the driver before starting your journey, especially if you're heading to a destination outside the town center.

- **Additional Charges:** Be aware that there might be extra charges for baggage, late-night rides, or holidays. These are typically indicated on the taxi's rate card, which the driver should have on display.

- **Tipping:** Tipping is appreciated but not mandatory. It's common to round up the fare to the nearest euro as a gesture of appreciation.

Hailing a Taxi:

- **Taxi Stands:** You can find taxi stands at prominent locations throughout the island, including the airport, the port, and the main towns. At these stands, you can easily hail a taxi, and there is usually a queue system.

- **Hand Signals:** If you're not near a taxi stand, you can flag down a taxi by raising your hand. Greek taxi drivers are accustomed to this method and will stop for you if they have availability.

Taxi Apps:

- Several taxi companies on the island offer smartphone apps that allow you to request a taxi with ease. These apps often provide a fare estimate and track the taxi's arrival in real-time.

Sample Taxi Fares:

To give you an idea of what to expect, here are some approximate taxi fares from popular locations:

- **Kos Airport to Kos Town:** Around €30 to €35
- **Kos Town to Tigaki:** Approximately €15 to €20
- **Kos Town to Asklepion:** Roughly €10 to €15

Please note that these fares are subject to change and may vary slightly depending on the time of day and the specific taxi company.

Taxi Services for Day Trips:

If you're interested in exploring multiple attractions or destinations in a single day, some taxi drivers offer guided day trips. These drivers can provide valuable insights and take you to the island's most iconic spots.

Taxis in Kos are a convenient, comfortable, and reliable means of transportation. Whether you're traveling solo, with a group, or just need a quick ride to your next destination, you can count on the island's taxi services to get you there efficiently and comfortably.

Buses

Buses are a convenient and budget-friendly mode of public transportation on the island of Kos. They offer an excellent way to explore the island, with well-organized routes and reliable schedules. Here, we delve into the details of the bus system, helping you make the most of this transportation option:

Bus Routes

The bus network on Kos covers most major towns, tourist destinations, and significant points of interest. Some of the primary routes include:

1. **Kos Town**: The capital and transportation hub, where you can easily catch a bus to various parts of the island.

2. **Kardamena**: A popular resort town on the southern coast with connections to many beaches and attractions.

3. **Mastichari**: Another seaside village with access to the beautiful Mastichari Beach and the harbor for ferry connections to Kalymnos and Pserimos.

4. **Tingaki**: Located on the northern coast, this area is known for its pristine beach and offers connections to other parts of the island.

5. **Kefalos**: A charming town on the southwest coast, serving as a gateway to some of the most beautiful beaches on the island.

Schedules and Timetables

Bus schedules on Kos are generally reliable, but it's advisable to check the timetables in advance, especially if you're planning a day trip. Buses usually run more frequently during the summer tourist season and may have reduced schedules in the off-season. Keep in mind that schedules may vary, so be prepared for minor adjustments.

Tickets and Fares

Purchasing tickets is straightforward. You can buy them from the bus driver as you board the bus. Fares are typically reasonable, making the bus an economical way to explore the island. There are often options for single-ride tickets, day passes, and multi-day passes, allowing you to choose the most cost-effective option for your travel plans.

Bus Stops

Bus stops on Kos are well-marked and easy to identify. They're usually found at central locations within towns, near popular tourist areas, and along main roads. Pay attention to the signs, and don't hesitate to ask locals for assistance if you're unsure about where to catch a bus.

Travel Tips

1. **Check Schedules**: Verify bus schedules in advance, especially during the off-season, to ensure you don't miss your ride.

2. **Be Early**: Arrive a few minutes early at the bus stop to guarantee your spot, as some routes may get crowded during peak hours.

3. **Exact Change**: If possible, carry small denominations of cash to pay for your bus fare. Drivers may not always have change for larger bills.

4. **Tourist Cards**: If you plan on using the bus extensively, consider purchasing a tourist card, which can offer discounts and convenience for multiple rides.

5. **Respect Others**: Be mindful of fellow passengers, and keep noise levels and personal belongings in check to ensure a pleasant journey for everyone.

Walking and Biking
Walking

Kos, with its relatively compact size and picturesque landscapes, is a paradise for walkers and hikers. Exploring the island on foot allows you to savor every detail of its natural beauty and historical significance.

Walking in Kos Town: Start your journey with a leisurely stroll in Kos Town. The town's charming streets are adorned with vibrant bougainvillea, making it an ideal place for a romantic evening walk. As you walk, you'll come across historical treasures such as the Ancient Agora, the Neratzia Castle, and the Hippocrates Tree, which provides lovely shade for a restful stop.

Walking along the Coast: Kos boasts a beautiful coastal path that stretches for miles. This walk offers stunning views of the crystal-clear Aegean Sea and is perfect for a morning jog, a romantic sunset stroll, or a peaceful escape from the bustling city.

Exploring Historical Sites: One of the most enriching ways to experience the island's history is by walking to its historical sites. Explore the Asklepion, an ancient healing center, and the ruins of the ancient city of Kos, which are scattered throughout the island's interior. These walks will not only take you through history but also immerse you in the island's tranquil countryside.

Hiking in the Mountains: If you're an avid hiker, head to the interior of Kos, where you'll find the Dikeos Mountain range. The ascent to Mount Dikeos offers breathtaking vistas and a taste of Kos's more rugged terrain. Remember to bring suitable hiking gear and plenty of water.

Guided Walking Tours: For those who want to delve deep into Kos's history and culture, consider joining a guided walking tour. Local guides can provide valuable insights into the island's past and its vibrant present.

Cycling

Kos's cycling infrastructure and inviting terrain make it an excellent destination for bike enthusiasts. Cycling provides a fantastic way to explore the island's diverse landscapes and discover hidden gems.

Cycling Paths: The island has an extensive network of dedicated cycling paths, making it safe and convenient to explore on two wheels. You can ride along the coast, through picturesque villages, and into the heart of the island's lush countryside.

Bicycle Rentals: Renting a bicycle is easy, with rental shops scattered across the island. You can choose from a variety of bikes, including mountain bikes for those who crave off-road adventures and comfortable city bikes for leisurely rides.

Exploring the Villages: Riding a bike allows you to venture into the charming villages that are often missed by tourists. Villages like Zia, Kardamena, and Antimachia offer a glimpse into traditional Greek life.

Group Cycling Tours: If you prefer a more social experience, consider joining a group cycling tour. These tours often include knowledgeable guides who can lead you to the island's most scenic spots and share local insights.

Respect Local Traffic Rules: While cycling is an enjoyable and eco-friendly way to get around, remember to adhere to local traffic rules and exercise caution, especially on busier roads.

Whether you choose to explore on foot or by bike, you'll be captivated by the natural beauty, historical charm, and warm hospitality of Kos. These methods of transportation allow you to experience the island at your own pace, creating memories that will last a lifetime. Enjoy the freedom and serenity that walking and cycling provide as you discover the hidden treasures of this stunning Greek island.

Trains

While trains are not the primary mode of transportation on the island of Kos, they do offer an interesting and unique way to explore specific parts of the island. Here, we will delve deeper into the limited train options available, providing you with insights into how to make the most of this mode of transport.

The Zia Train

The Zia Train is a charming and nostalgic attraction for both locals and tourists. It's not your typical commuter train; rather, it's a small, vintage-style train that offers a delightful journey through some of Kos's picturesque countryside.

Route: The Zia Train typically follows a circular route, departing from the village of Zia and making its way through the scenic hills and villages of the island's interior. The journey provides passengers with breathtaking views of the lush landscapes, olive groves, and charming Greek villages.

Scenic Stops: Along the way, the train may make brief stops at points of interest, including small villages, local craft shops, and picturesque viewpoints. This allows you to disembark, explore, and take in the natural beauty of Kos.

Duration and Schedule: The Zia Train journey is usually relatively short, lasting around 45 minutes to 1 hour. The schedule may vary seasonally, so it's advisable to check the departure times in advance.

What to Expect

- **Nostalgic Experience**: Riding the Zia Train is like stepping back in time. The vintage design of the train cars and the slow, leisurely pace of the journey create a nostalgic atmosphere.

- **Scenic Views**: The train's route is carefully selected to showcase the island's stunning landscapes, making it an excellent choice for photographers and nature enthusiasts.

- **Local Culture**: During your journey, you may have the chance to interact with locals at the stops, providing you with a glimpse into the authentic Greek island lifestyle.

Practical Tips

- **Check the Schedule**: As the schedule can change, it's wise to verify the departure times and availability of the Zia Train before planning your trip.

- **Tickets**: Tickets are typically affordable and can be purchased at the train station or in advance online.

- **Camera Ready**: Don't forget your camera or smartphone – you'll want to capture the breathtaking scenery along the way.

- **Comfortable Clothing**: Wear comfortable clothing and suitable footwear, especially if you plan to disembark and explore at the stops.

While trains are not a comprehensive mode of transport on Kos, the Zia Train offers a unique and memorable way to experience the island's natural beauty and local culture. Whether you're traveling with family, friends, or on your own, a ride on the Zia Train can be a delightful addition to your Kos adventure.

Ferries and Boats

Kos, situated in the Dodecanese island group of Greece, is a perfect starting point for exploring other nearby islands and the stunning Aegean Sea. Ferries and boats play a crucial role in connecting Kos to these neighboring destinations, making island-hopping and sea adventures an integral part of your Kos experience.

Ferry Routes

Kos has multiple ferry routes departing from its main harbor. These routes offer access to a variety of nearby islands, each with its own unique charm. Some of the most popular ferry routes from Kos include:

- **Rhodes**: The short distance to Rhodes, one of the largest and most historically significant islands in the Dodecanese, makes it a common choice for day trips or longer stays.

- **Kalymnos**: Famous for its natural beauty, Kalymnos is a haven for rock climbers and water sports enthusiasts. Ferries to Kalymnos provide opportunities for exciting adventures.

- **Patmos**: Known for its religious and historical significance, Patmos attracts pilgrims and history buffs. The ferry journey to Patmos offers breathtaking views of the Aegean.

- **Symi**: With its charming neoclassical architecture, Symi is a picturesque island worth exploring. Ferries to Symi make it a popular day trip destination.

- **Bodrum (Turkey)**: For a touch of international flair, you can take a ferry to Bodrum, Turkey, which is in close proximity to Kos.

Ferry Operators

Several ferry operators serve the routes from Kos to neighboring islands. Some of the prominent ferry companies include:

- **Blue Star Ferries**: Offering reliable and comfortable services, Blue Star Ferries connect Kos with several Dodecanese islands.

- **Dodekanisos Seaways**: This company specializes in connecting the islands of the Dodecanese, including Kos, with fast and efficient catamarans.

- **Aegean Speed Lines**: Ideal for travelers looking for speed and convenience, Aegean Speed Lines offer high-speed ferry services to various destinations.

Ticket Booking

To make your island-hopping experience smooth and hassle-free, you can book your ferry tickets in advance. Here are some tips for booking your ferry tickets:

- **Online Booking**: Many ferry companies offer online booking services, allowing you to reserve your tickets before you arrive in Kos.

- **Local Ticket Offices**: You can also purchase tickets from local ticket offices in Kos Town and other major towns on the island.

- **Travel Agencies**: Travel agencies in Kos often provide ticket booking services, including guidance on ferry schedules and routes.

Ferry Schedules

Ferry schedules vary depending on the season, with more frequent departures during the summer months. It's advisable to check the schedules in advance and consider booking your tickets early during peak travel periods.

Exploring the Aegean

Ferries and boats are not just a means of transportation; they are also a gateway to exciting adventures. While aboard, you can enjoy the beauty of the Aegean Sea, its crystal-clear waters, and the picturesque islands you pass by. Don't forget to bring your camera to capture the stunning scenery and seascapes.

CHAPTER THREE

ACCOMMODATION OPTION IN KOS

When planning your trip to Kos, one of the most crucial decisions you'll make is where to stay. The island offers a diverse range of accommodation options to suit all preferences and budgets. From luxury resorts to budget-friendly hostels, Kos has it all.

Types of Accommodation

Choosing the right accommodation is a pivotal decision in planning your trip to any destination, and Kos is no exception. The island offers a diverse array of lodging options to cater to various preferences and budgets. In this section, we'll delve into the different types of accommodation you can find on the beautiful island of Kos.

Hotels

Hotels are among the most popular and versatile forms of accommodation on the enchanting island of Kos. From the simplicity of family-run inns to the lavishness of beachfront resorts, Kos's hotel offerings cater to travelers with diverse preferences and budgets. This section explores the world of hotels on the island and provides insights into what you can expect when staying in one.

Variety of Hotels

One of the key reasons why hotels are a preferred choice for many travelers to Kos is the sheer variety available. Whether you're looking for a cozy and affordable stay or a luxurious retreat, the island's hotels have got you covered.

Features:

- **Budget-Friendly Options:** Kos offers a range of budget-friendly hotels, providing comfortable and clean rooms without breaking the bank. These are ideal for travelers looking for affordability without compromising on comfort. **Hotel Seaside Haven**, a budget-friendly hotel located just a stone's throw away from the pristine beaches of Kos

- **Mid-Range Comfort:** For those who desire a balance between price and comfort, mid-range hotels on the island provide quality service and amenities. **Olive Grove Hotel** is one of such hotel.

- **Luxurious Retreats:** If you're in search of a lavish vacation, Kos boasts luxurious beachfront resorts with world-class facilities, private beaches, and stunning sea views**. Astir Odysseus Kos Resort and Spa** is one of such accommodation.

- **Family-Friendly Hotels:** Many hotels on the island are designed with families in mind, offering amenities like children's clubs, pool areas, and entertainment options to keep kids happy. **SunSplash Hotel** is one of such hotel.

Hotel Amenities

Hotels on Kos offer an array of amenities to enhance your stay and provide a comfortable and memorable experience.

Common Amenities:

- **Swimming Pools:** Many hotels, especially in the mid-range and luxury categories, have swimming pools where you can relax and cool off.

- **On-Site Dining:** Most hotels feature on-site restaurants and bars, serving local and international cuisine. This convenience is perfect for days when you'd rather not venture far.

- **Room Service:** For added convenience, hotels often offer room service, allowing you to enjoy meals in the privacy of your room or suite.

- **Daily Housekeeping:** Housekeeping services ensure that your room remains clean and tidy throughout your stay.

- **Wi-Fi:** In the digital age, staying connected is essential. Many hotels offer complimentary Wi-Fi, though the speed and coverage may vary.

Location and Accessibility

The strategic locations of hotels on the island are a crucial factor to consider when booking your stay. Proximity to the island's attractions, beaches, and town centers can significantly enhance your experience.

Key Considerations:

- **Kos Town:** If you prefer to be at the heart of the action, staying in Kos Town, the island's capital, is an excellent choice. It offers easy access to historical sites, shops, and the lively nightlife.

- **Kardamena:** Located on the southern coast, Kardamena is known for its vibrant nightlife and beautiful beaches. Ideal for those who seek lively evenings and sunny days on the beach.

- **Tigaki:** On the northern coast, Tigaki offers a more tranquil atmosphere with stunning beaches, making it perfect for families and couples seeking a peaceful retreat.

- **Mastichari:** In the northwest, Mastichari is a tranquil fishing village with pristine beaches, providing an authentic and peaceful Greek experience.

- **Charming Villages:** Throughout the island, there are charming villages like Zia and Pyli, which offer a unique and tranquil setting away from the tourist crowds.

Tip: When selecting your hotel, think about what type of experience you desire during your stay, whether it's vibrant nightlife, serene beaches, or an authentic local atmosphere.

Overall, choosing the right hotel in Kos can significantly impact your overall travel experience.

Online hotel booking can be done on websites like **booking.com** and to check reviews of different hotels accommodation **tripadvisor.com** is a good resource for that.

Apartments and Villas

Apartments and villas are popular choices of accommodation on the island of Kos. Offering a more private and independent experience, these lodging options are perfect for families, groups, or anyone seeking a home-away-from-home feel. In this section, we'll delve into what you can expect when choosing apartments and villas as your Kos retreat.

Why Choose Apartments and Villas

1. Space and Comfort

Apartments and villas provide more space than traditional hotel rooms. This extra room is a blessing for larger groups or families, allowing everyone to spread out and relax. You'll often have separate bedrooms, living areas, and fully equipped kitchens, offering a level of comfort that hotels can't always match.

2. Self-Catering Facilities

One of the significant advantages of staying in an apartment or villa is the presence of a kitchen. You can prepare your meals, which is not only a cost-saving option but also allows you to experience local cuisine by visiting markets and experimenting with local ingredients. It's a chance to dine on your own schedule, whether that means having a leisurely breakfast or a late-night snack.

3. Privacy and Freedom

Staying in apartments or villas provides a level of privacy that's hard to find in hotels. You won't have to worry about noisy neighbors in the room next door. You'll have your own space to unwind after a day of exploring Kos. Whether you're enjoying a quiet evening on the terrace, taking a dip in your private pool, or having a barbecue, you'll have the freedom to make the most of your time on your own terms.

4. Local Experience

Apartments and villas are often situated in residential neighborhoods, giving you a taste of local life. You'll have the opportunity to interact with locals, shop at neighborhood markets, and immerse yourself in the culture of Kos in a way that hotels in tourist areas might not offer. This can add depth to your travel experience and allow you to discover hidden gems.

Choosing the Right Apartment or Villa

Budget: Apartments and villas in Kos come in a range of prices to suit different budgets. Higher-end options might include private pools, stunning views, and premium furnishings, while more budget-friendly choices can provide a comfortable, no-frills experience.

Location: Consider the location carefully. Do you want to be near the beach, close to the town center, or in a quiet village? Research the surrounding area to ensure it meets your preferences for accessibility to attractions and activities.

Size and Amenities: Check the size and amenities offered. Depending on your group size and preferences, you may want multiple bedrooms, a private pool, or a sea view. Read property descriptions and guest reviews to get a clear idea of what's included.

Booking Platforms: There are numerous booking platforms and rental agencies where you can find apartments and villas on Kos. Popular options include Airbnb, Booking.com, HomeAway, and local agencies. Be sure to read reviews, verify property details, and confirm booking conditions before finalizing your reservation.

Tips for a Great Stay

1. **Communication:** Contact the property owner or manager before your trip to clarify any questions or special requests.

2. **Local Markets:** Make the most of your kitchen by shopping at local markets for fresh ingredients and regional specialties.

3. **Transport:** Consider renting a car or bike for easy access to the island's attractions, especially if your villa is in a more remote area.

4. **Safety:** Always ensure that your accommodation is secure, especially when leaving valuables behind.

Overall, choosing an apartment or villa for your stay in Kos offers a unique and personal way to experience the island.

Hostels

Hostels are lodging establishments that cater to travelers on a budget. They typically feature dormitory-style rooms with bunk beds, though some may also offer private rooms. Hostels are designed to encourage social interaction among guests, making them an excellent choice for solo travelers, backpackers, and those seeking a communal atmosphere.

Key Features:

- **Affordability:** Hostels are known for their cost-effective accommodation options, making them an attractive choice for travelers on a tight budget.

- **Social Atmosphere:** Hostels often provide common areas, communal kitchens, and organized activities to foster interaction among guests.

- **Dormitory-Style Rooms:** While dormitories are the norm, many hostels offer private rooms for those who value a bit more privacy.

- **Basic Amenities:** Though simpler than hotels, hostels usually provide essential facilities such as shared bathrooms, Wi-Fi, and common areas for relaxation and dining.

Tip

- If you're not keen on sharing a room with strangers, consider booking a private room in a hostel, which offers a more hotel-like experience.

Advantages of Staying in Hostels

Affordability: Hostels are often the most budget-friendly accommodation option, allowing travelers to save money on lodging and allocate their budget to experiences and activities.

Social Interaction: Hostels provide an excellent environment for meeting fellow travelers from around the world. It's a great way to make new friends, share travel stories, and possibly find travel companions.

Local Insights: Hostel staff and fellow travelers can provide valuable insights into the local culture, hidden gems, and off-the-beaten-path experiences.

Flexible Booking: Many hostels offer flexible booking options, allowing you to stay for just one night or extend your visit if you decide to explore the island further.

Organized Activities: Some hostels organize group activities, tours, and events, which can enhance your overall travel experience.

Tip: Check online reviews and ratings to choose a hostel that aligns with your expectations and travel style.

What to Expect When Staying in a Hostel

Dormitory Rooms: Most hostels offer dormitory-style rooms with bunk beds, typically separated by gender. Each bed typically comes with its locker to secure your valuables.

Shared Facilities: Hostels provide shared bathrooms, which are usually clean and well-maintained. Communal kitchens are also available for guests to prepare their meals.

Lockers and Security: Hostels have lockers or safes for securing your valuables. It's essential to bring a padlock for these lockers.

Social Areas: Common areas like lounges, bars, and outdoor spaces are designed for socializing and meeting fellow travelers.

Wi-Fi: Free Wi-Fi is standard in most hostels, allowing you to stay connected with friends and family or plan your next adventures.

Local Knowledge: Hostel staff are typically well-informed about the local area and can provide recommendations for things to do, places to eat, and how to get around.

Tips for Staying in Hostels

- **Pack Light:** Hostel rooms might have limited space, so pack only the essentials.
- **Bring Earplugs:** Dormitory-style rooms can get noisy, so earplugs can help ensure a good night's sleep.

- **Respect Others:** Maintain a quiet and respectful demeanor in communal areas and dormitories, especially during late hours.
- **Hygiene:** Bring your toiletries, including a towel and shower sandals. Hostels may provide these items, but it's best to have your own.
- **Socialize:** Don't be shy; take advantage of the social atmosphere to meet new people and possibly find travel companions.

Staying in a hostel on Kos is not just a way to save money; it's an opportunity to immerse yourself in a dynamic and sociable travel community.

All-Inclusive Resorts

When it comes to ultimate relaxation and convenience, all-inclusive resorts in Kos, Greece, are hard to beat. These resorts offer a hassle-free vacation experience where almost everything you need is included in one upfront price. In this section, we'll explore the world of all-inclusive resorts and why they might be the perfect choice for your stay in Kos.

What Are All-Inclusive Resorts?

All-inclusive resorts are holiday destinations where the price you pay for your stay covers not only your accommodation but also a wide range of services and amenities. These typically include meals, drinks, entertainment, activities, and sometimes even airport transfers. Essentially, once you check in, you can leave your wallet behind.

Benefits of Choosing an All-Inclusive Resort in Kos

Convenience: One of the primary reasons travelers choose all-inclusive resorts is the sheer convenience they offer. You won't need to worry about planning meals or searching for places to eat, as breakfast, lunch, dinner, and snacks are all included. This convenience is especially appealing for families, as it minimizes the stress of catering to various dietary preferences.

Value for Money: While the initial cost of booking an all-inclusive resort might appear high, it can actually save you money in the long run. When you consider the expenses of dining out, entertainment, and activities, you'll often find that the all-inclusive package provides excellent value. Plus, it allows you to budget more accurately.

Variety of Dining Options: All-inclusive resorts in Kos typically offer a range of dining options, from buffet-style meals to à la carte restaurants specializing in various cuisines. This variety ensures that you won't grow tired of the food offerings during your stay. Some resorts also offer 24-hour room service, making it easy to satisfy late-night cravings.

Activities and Entertainment: In addition to meals, all-inclusive packages often include an array of recreational activities and entertainment options. These may include water sports, fitness facilities, live shows, and more. It's an excellent choice for travelers who like to stay active and engaged during their vacation.

Family-Friendly: Many all-inclusive resorts in Kos cater to families with children, offering kids' clubs, supervised activities, and family-friendly entertainment. This makes them an ideal choice for those traveling with kids, as parents can relax while their children are engaged and supervised.

What's Included in All-Inclusive Packages?

The inclusions in all-inclusive packages can vary from one resort to another, but here are some common items covered:

- **Meals:** Breakfast, lunch, dinner, and snacks.

- **Drinks:** Alcoholic and non-alcoholic beverages, including local and international brands.

- **Activities:** Access to pools, fitness centers, and various recreational activities.

- **Entertainment:** Evening shows, live music, and themed events.

- **Children's Activities:** Kids' clubs, games, and supervised programs.

- **Water Sports:** Non-motorized water sports like kayaking and snorkeling.

- **Airport Transfers:** Some resorts include airport transfers for added convenience.

Examples of All-Inclusive Resorts in Kos:

1. Mitsis Blue Domes Resort & Spa

- **Location:** Kardamena, Kos

- **Key Features:** This 5-star resort offers luxurious rooms, numerous restaurants, a private beach, and a world-class spa. It's a family-friendly destination with dedicated pools for both adults and children.

2. Ikos Aria

- **Location:** Kefalos, Kos

- **Key Features:** This upscale, award-winning resort is renowned for its stunning beachfront setting, Michelin-starred restaurants, and a vast array of activities, including watersports and theater performances.

3. Grecotel Kos Imperial Thalasso

- **Location:** Psalidi, Kos
- **Key Features:** Nestled along the beach, this resort offers a lavish thalassotherapy center, beautiful gardens, multiple dining options, and family-friendly amenities like waterslides and a kids' club.

4. TUI BLUE Atlantica Belvedere Resort

- **Location:** Kardamena, Kos
- **Key Features:** This contemporary resort provides a serene ambiance, numerous dining choices, wellness facilities, and access to a stunning beach. It's perfect for couples seeking a romantic escape.

5. LTI Louis Grand Hotel

- **Location:** Kardamena, Kos
- **Key Features:** A family-oriented resort with a private beach, several pools, sports facilities, and diverse dining options, including a Greek taverna.

Tips for Choosing an All-Inclusive Resort in Kos

- **Research Thoroughly:** Read reviews, browse resort websites, and consult travel forums to find the resort that aligns with your preferences and budget.

- **Check the Fine Print:** Make sure you understand what's included and what's not. Some activities and premium dining options may come at an extra cost.

- **Consider the Location:** Think about what kind of environment you want. Do you prefer a beachfront resort, something closer to town, or a more secluded option?

- **Family or Adults-Only:** Depending on your travel group, some resorts are adults-only, while others are family-friendly. Choose accordingly.

- **Book in Advance:** All-inclusive resorts can get busy, especially during peak tourist seasons. Booking well in advance ensures you secure your desired dates.

Overall, All-inclusive resorts in Kos are an excellent choice for travelers seeking a hassle-free and value-packed vacation.

Campsites

When it comes to experiencing the pristine beauty of Kos while being immersed in nature, camping is a unique and budget-friendly option that promises an unforgettable adventure. The island offers several campsites where you can set up your tent, park your camper, or even rent a pre-equipped tent, allowing you to connect with the great outdoors in a truly Greek paradise.

Why Camp in Kos?

Camping on the island of Kos offers a range of benefits and experiences that are hard to match with other types of accommodation. Here's why you should consider camping:

Scenic Locations: Kos boasts an array of scenic camping sites, many of which are nestled along the coast, providing breathtaking views of the Aegean Sea. Waking up to the sound of gentle waves and the sight of the sun rising over the water is an experience you won't forget.

Affordability: Camping is one of the most budget-friendly accommodation options on the island. You'll save money on lodging, which can then be spent on exploring the island's attractions or enjoying local cuisine.

Outdoor Experience: Camping allows you to connect with nature and appreciate the island's natural beauty up close. Spend your days hiking, swimming, or simply basking in the Mediterranean sun, and your nights stargazing by the campfire.

Social Atmosphere: Campsites are often social hubs where travelers from around the world come together. It's an excellent opportunity to meet like-minded adventurers and share travel stories.

Campsite Options

Kos offers a selection of campsites, each with its own charm and features. Here are a few popular ones to consider:

Camping Kos

- **Location:** Kefalos, southwest Kos.
- **Highlights:** A beautiful, well-organized campsite with modern facilities, offering direct access to the beach and water sports.
- **Amenities:** Showers, toilets, a restaurant, and mini-market.

Marmari Beach Campsite

- **Location:** Marmari, north Kos.
- **Highlights:** Situated in a peaceful location near the beach, perfect for water sports enthusiasts and nature lovers.
- **Amenities:** Showers, toilets, a restaurant, and a supermarket.

Bubble Luxotel

- **Location:** Tigaki, northeast Kos.

- **Highlights:** A unique camping experience with pre-set "bubble tents" for stargazing from the comfort of your bed.

- **Amenities:** Showers, toilets, and a beach bar.

Tips for Camping in Kos

To make the most of your camping adventure in Kos, here are some essential tips to keep in mind:

- **Check Campsite Rules:** Each campsite may have its own set of rules and regulations, such as quiet hours, campfire policies, and waste disposal guidelines. Be sure to familiarize yourself with these to ensure a pleasant stay.
- **Equipment and Supplies:** Pack essential camping gear, including a tent, sleeping bag, camping stove, and other necessities. If you're not bringing your gear, check whether the campsite offers equipment rentals.
- **Weather Preparedness:** Kos experiences a Mediterranean climate with hot, dry summers and mild winters. Ensure your camping gear is suitable for the prevailing weather conditions during your visit.
- **Respect Nature:** As a responsible camper, always respect the natural environment. Leave no trace,

pick up your trash, and avoid disturbing local wildlife.

- **Security:** While camping is generally safe, it's wise to take precautions. Keep your belongings secure and be aware of your surroundings.

Overall, camping in Kos allows you to explore the island in a unique and immersive way.

In conclusion, choosing the right type of accommodation in Kos depends on your travel style, budget, and preferences. Whether you opt for a luxurious beachfront resort, a cozy apartment, or a camping adventure, Kos offers something for every traveler. Remember to book in advance during peak tourist seasons to secure your ideal lodging.

CHAPTER FOUR

TOP ATTRACTIONS

Kos offers a wide array of attractions that cater to every traveler's interests. From ancient archaeological sites to natural wonders and vibrant nightlife, here's a comprehensive guide to the top attractions on this stunning Greek island.

Historical Sites

Kos is a treasure trove of historical sites that will transport you back in time. These ancient relics and monuments offer an invaluable glimpse into the island's rich history and heritage. As you explore these historical sites, consider these important details for a truly enriching experience.

Asclepius Sanctuary (Asklepion)
Location: South   of   Kos   Town
Opening Hours: 8:00 AM - 6:00 PM

The Asclepius Sanctuary, also known as Asklepion, stands as a remarkable testament to the ancient world's reverence for healing and medicine. Situated to the south of Kos Town, this historical site is a must-visit for travelers seeking to delve into the island's rich past and its deep connections to medicine and spirituality.

History and Significance

Asklepion was not merely a medical facility; it was a sacred space dedicated to Asclepius, the Greek god of healing and medicine. This center of holistic health was established around the 4th century BC and rapidly gained fame for its unique approach to well-being.

Key Points for Travelers:

1. **Ancient Healing Traditions**: At Asklepion, ancient Greeks practiced holistic healing, blending elements of religion, philosophy, and medicine. The site includes a sacred spring where patients would cleanse themselves, symbolizing the purification of both body and soul.

2. **Learning and Meditation**: In addition to treating the sick, Asklepion served as a place of learning and meditation. Visitors, including famous historical figures like Hippocrates, would engage in discussions, gain insights, and develop a profound understanding of medicine and philosophy.

3. **Architectural Marvel**: The site's layout is a marvel in itself, featuring terraces, courtyards, colonnades, and temples. As you explore, the layout offers an excellent vantage point to take in panoramic views of the surrounding landscape.

What to See and Do

When you visit Asklepion, there are several key attractions and activities that can enrich your experience:

1. **The Three Terraces**: As you ascend the terraces, you'll encounter various structures and monuments, including the Temple of Asclepius, the Doric Stoa, and the famous tholos, a circular building that once housed the famous statue of Asclepius.

2. **Ancient Theater**: Discover the theater, which once hosted discussions and performances, adding an artistic dimension to the site.

3. **Panoramic Views**: Take a moment to appreciate the breathtaking views of the island and the Aegean Sea, offering a serene atmosphere for reflection.

Tips for Travelers

- **Guided Tours**: Consider taking a guided tour to gain a deeper understanding of the history, culture, and medical practices of the ancient world.

- **Wear Comfortable Shoes**: The site involves a fair amount of walking and ascending terraces, so wear comfortable footwear.

- **Bring Water and Sun Protection**: The Mediterranean sun can be quite strong. Ensure you have adequate sun protection and stay hydrated during your visit.

- **Respect the Site**: Please be mindful of the historical significance of this site and show respect for its heritage by not defacing or disturbing the ruins.

A visit to the Asclepius Sanctuary is more than just exploring historical ruins; it's an opportunity to connect with the ancient world's approach to health and well-being. As you wander through the terraces and courtyards, you'll feel the echoes of history and the enduring quest for healing, making your trip to Kos even more enriching and memorable.

Ancient Agora of Kos

Location: Kos Town
Opening Hours: 8:00 AM - 6:00 PM (may vary seasonally)

The Ancient Agora of Kos, nestled in the heart of Kos Town, is a historical and archaeological gem that offers a window into the island's rich past. This site is a must-visit for history enthusiasts, culture seekers, and anyone looking to immerse themselves in the fascinating heritage of Kos.

Historical Significance:

The Ancient Agora was the bustling hub of ancient Kos and played a pivotal role in the island's social, political, and economic life. Here's what you need to know:

- **Marketplace and Beyond:** The Agora served as both a bustling marketplace and a central meeting place for political discussions, cultural events, and social gatherings.

- **Greek History:** Dating back to the 4th century BC, the Agora's history is intertwined with the rich tapestry of ancient Greek civilization.

Exploring the Site:

As you wander through this historical site, be sure to:

- **Temple of Hercules**: Marvel at the well-preserved Temple of Hercules, an iconic Doric-style temple dedicated to the mythological hero.

- **Bouleuterion:** Discover the Bouleuterion, an ancient council chamber where important decisions were made in the political life of the city.

- **Odeon:** The Odeon, a small theater, speaks to the cultural life of ancient Kos, hosting musical and theatrical performances.

- **Stoas and Columns:** The Agora is dotted with stoa remains (colonnades) and numerous columns, providing a captivating backdrop for your exploration.

Interactive Experience:

The Ancient Agora of Kos is not just an archaeological site; it's a dynamic place that often hosts cultural events and exhibitions. Here's how to make the most of your visit:

- **Cultural Events:** Keep an eye out for any ongoing cultural events, such as art exhibitions, musical performances, or theater productions. These events breathe life into the ancient stones and offer a unique, immersive experience.

- **Local Insights:** Engage with knowledgeable guides or fellow travelers to gain a deeper understanding of the historical context and significance of the site.

- **Photography Opportunity:** Don't forget your camera! The well-preserved ruins against the backdrop of the Aegean Sea create a photographer's paradise.

The Ancient Agora of Kos is not just a static historical site; it's a living testament to the vibrant past of the island.

Castle of the Knights (Neratzia Castle)
Location: Kos Town

Opening Hours: 8:00 AM - 8:00 PM

Neratzia Castle, also known as the Castle of the Knights, is a medieval fortress that stands as a testament to the rich history of Kos. This captivating castle, with its imposing walls, drawbridges, and medieval charm, is a must-visit for history enthusiasts and anyone seeking to delve into the island's intriguing past.

A Glimpse into History

- **Knights of Saint John**: The Castle of the Knights was constructed in the 14th century by the Knights of Saint John, a religious and military order. This monumental fortress was built to protect the island from invaders and pirates, making it a vital part of Kos's history.

- **Imposing Architecture**: The castle's imposing architecture reflects a time when fortified structures were essential for security. Its sturdy walls and well-preserved bastions are a remarkable example of medieval fortifications.

Exploring the Castle

- **Drawbridges and Moats**: As you approach the castle, you'll cross a drawbridge over a picturesque moat. The moat was not only a defensive feature but also served as a source of fresh water for the knights.

- **Towers and Courtyards**: Within the castle, you'll discover various towers, courtyards, and chambers that once housed knights and their supplies. Climb the towers for panoramic views of the surrounding area, including Kos Town and the harbor.

- **Summer Events**: In the summer months, the castle often hosts cultural events and exhibitions. These events provide an opportunity to experience the historical and cultural aspects of the castle in a dynamic way.

Tips for Visitors

- **Guided Tours**: Consider taking a guided tour of the castle to gain a deeper understanding of its history, architecture, and the knights who once called it home. Knowledgeable guides can bring the past to life with intriguing stories.

- **Photography**: The castle's architecture and the views it offers make it a paradise for photography enthusiasts. Don't forget to bring your camera or smartphone to capture the magic of this medieval fortress.

- **Accessibility**: While the castle is a historically significant site, it might not be accessible for visitors with mobility issues due to stairs and uneven terrain. Please plan your visit accordingly.

A visit to the Castle of the Knights (Neratzia Castle) is a journey through time, allowing you to immerse yourself in the medieval history of Kos. Explore the impressive architecture, admire the panoramic vistas, and let your imagination roam as you step back into a world of knights, fortifications, and island legends.

Natural Wonders

Kos, with its Mediterranean charm, offers a plethora of natural wonders that will captivate any traveler's heart. From relaxing hot springs to breathtaking mountaintop vistas, this section is your guide to experiencing the island's most remarkable natural attractions.

Therma Beach

Location: Agios Fokas, Kos

Nestled along the southern coast of Kos, Therma Beach is a hidden treasure of natural beauty and tranquility. What sets this beach apart from the others on the island is its remarkable natural hot springs. Travelers flock to Therma Beach to immerse themselves in its warm, therapeutic waters, which have gained a reputation for their healing properties. This chapter offers a comprehensive guide to Therma Beach, highlighting its unique features and what you can expect when you visit.

The Warm Waters: The defining feature of Therma Beach is its naturally heated waters. These thermal springs are a gift from the island's volcanic activity, and the mineral-rich content of the water is believed to have a variety of health benefits. As you step into the sea, you'll immediately feel the warmth enveloping you. The sensation is incredibly soothing and makes for a unique beach experience.

Scenic Views: Besides the warm waters, Therma Beach offers stunning panoramic views of the Aegean Sea. The cove is surrounded by rocky cliffs and lush vegetation, creating a serene and picturesque backdrop for your relaxation. Whether you're soaking in the hot springs or lounging on the pebble beach, you'll be treated to breathtaking vistas that add to the overall ambiance.

Sustainable Experience: One of the most remarkable aspects of Therma Beach is its natural and eco-friendly atmosphere. Unlike some commercialized beach destinations, Therma maintains a more rustic and authentic feel. The lack of overdevelopment adds to the sense of escaping into nature, making it an ideal spot for those looking to unwind and reconnect with the environment.

Traveler Tips:

- **Arrive Early:** Therma Beach can get quite popular, especially during peak tourist season. If you're seeking a more peaceful experience, consider visiting early in the morning when the crowds are thinner.

- **Footwear:** The seabed at Therma Beach is rocky, so bringing water shoes is advisable to protect your feet while entering the warm springs.

- **Camera Ready:** Don't forget your camera or smartphone – the surroundings are ideal for capturing memories. The dramatic landscape and crystal-clear waters provide excellent photo opportunities.

- **Relax and Rejuvenate:** While at Therma Beach, take your time to truly relax. The warm waters have a calming effect on the mind and body, making it an excellent opportunity to unwind and recharge.

Therma Beach on Kos is a natural wonder, offering an experience that combines relaxation and wellness.

Mount Dikaios

Location: Kos Island, Greece

Description: Mount Dikaios, the highest peak on Kos Island, is a pristine natural wonder that beckons travelers with its unparalleled beauty and countless opportunities for exploration. This chapter is your comprehensive guide to Mount Dikaios, where you can immerse yourself in nature and experience breathtaking views, serene hikes, and a rich variety of flora and fauna.

Why Visit Mount Dikaios:

1. Hiking Paradise

Mount Dikaios is a hiker's dream. With well-marked trails catering to various levels of expertise, it offers diverse hiking experiences. Whether you're a seasoned mountaineer or a beginner, there's a trail for you. The trails take you through lush forests, open meadows, and rocky terrains, promising a sense of adventure and a deeper connection with nature.

- **Trails for All:** Choose from easy, moderate, and challenging trails, making it accessible for hikers of all levels. The routes range from short walks to full-day excursions.

- **Awe-Inspiring Scenery:** While trekking, you'll be treated to stunning vistas, including panoramic views of Kos Island, neighboring islands, and the Turkish coast. The peak's elevation provides unparalleled perspectives of the Aegean Sea and the island's coastline.

2. Flora and Fauna

Mount Dikaios is not just a feast for the eyes; it's a botanical wonderland. The mountain's diverse range of Mediterranean plant life, including aromatic herbs like thyme and oregano, will envelop you in a fragrant embrace. While exploring the mountain, you may also encounter local wildlife, such as goats and numerous bird species, creating a harmonious ecosystem.

- **Botanical Diversity:** Take the opportunity to observe a wide variety of plants, including wildflowers and shrubs that add vibrant colors to the landscape.

- **Wildlife Encounters:** Keep your eyes peeled for resident wildlife. Birdwatchers may spot various bird species soaring in the sky or perched on rocky outcrops.

3. Unforgettable Sunsets

A visit to Mount Dikaios is not complete without witnessing a sunset from its summit. As the day draws to a close, the sky is painted in hues of pink, orange, and purple. It's a magical experience that will etch itself into your memory forever.

- **Photography Heaven:** Bring your camera to capture the mesmerizing play of colors as the sun sets over the Aegean Sea.

- **Romantic Escapade:** If you're visiting with a loved one, a sunset hike is the perfect romantic experience.

Traveler Tips:

- **Footwear:** Wear sturdy hiking boots or trail shoes with good grip to navigate the sometimes rocky and uneven terrain comfortably.

- **Hydration:** It's essential to carry enough water and snacks with you, as there are limited facilities on the mountain.

- **Binoculars:** Don't forget binoculars if you're into birdwatching; Mount Dikaios is a fantastic spot for observing avian wildlife.

- **Sunscreen and Layers:** Depending on the season, don't forget sunscreen and clothing layers to protect yourself from the sun or unexpected weather changes.

Getting There: Mount Dikaios is easily accessible by car from various points on Kos Island. It's a scenic drive through picturesque villages and beautiful landscapes, making the journey itself an enjoyable part of your adventure.

A visit to Mount Dikaios promises an authentic natural experience, where you can escape the hustle and bustle of modern life and reconnect with the tranquil beauty of the outdoors.

Kefalos Beach

Location: Kefalos, Kos

Description: Kefalos Beach is the epitome of a Greek island paradise. Situated on the southwest coast of Kos, this stunning beach is a magnet for visitors seeking a blend of relaxation, water sports, and exquisite natural beauty. Here's everything you need to know about this slice of heaven:

Golden Sands and Crystal-Clear Waters: Kefalos Beach boasts long stretches of soft, golden sands that gently slope into the crystal-clear waters of the Aegean Sea. The beach is exceptionally family-friendly, making it the perfect place for sunbathing, swimming, and building sandcastles with the kids.

Water Sports Adventure: For the more adventurous traveler, Kefalos Beach offers an array of thrilling water sports. From windsurfing to jet skiing, parasailing to paddleboarding, there's no shortage of opportunities to infuse your beach day with excitement. The consistent offshore winds make it an ideal spot for windsurfing and kiteboarding.

Tavernas and Cafes: Surrounding the beach, you'll find a charming collection of traditional tavernas and cafes. These establishments offer delectable Greek cuisine and a range of refreshing beverages, making it easy to savor local flavors while enjoying picturesque seafront views. Don't miss the chance to sample fresh seafood and Mediterranean specialties.

Scenic Backdrops: The beauty of Kefalos Beach extends beyond the shoreline. The area is graced with dramatic cliffs and hills, creating a picturesque backdrop that's perfect for leisurely strolls and photography. The sight of the sun setting over the Aegean is a spectacle not to be missed.

Traveler Tips:

- **Sun Protection:** The Mediterranean sun can be intense, so remember to pack sunscreen, a wide-brimmed hat, and a pair of sunglasses to protect yourself from UV rays.

- **Water Activities:** If you're eager to try water sports, inquire about equipment rentals and lessons at one of the beachside water sports centers.

- **Visit Times:** To avoid the midday crowds and the heat, consider visiting Kefalos Beach either in the morning or during the late afternoon.

- **Beach Facilities:** Kefalos Beach is equipped with sunbeds and umbrellas available for rent, so you can comfortably spend hours on the beach.

- **Explore the Area:** After a day at Kefalos Beach, take some time to explore the charming village of Kefalos, which is steeped in tradition and offers a glimpse into the local way of life.

Kefalos Beach on Kos is a true gem of the Aegean, where you can unwind in the sun, revel in exciting water activities, and savor delicious Greek cuisine.

Museums and Art Galleries

Kos is not only known for its stunning natural landscapes and historical sites but also for its rich cultural heritage. Museums and art galleries on the island offer an enlightening journey through history, art, and local culture.

Kos Archaeological Museum

Location: Kos Town

The Kos Archaeological Museum, situated in the heart of Kos Town, is a captivating cultural institution that stands as a testament to the island's rich history and heritage. As a traveler exploring Kos, a visit to this museum is a must to unlock the secrets of the island's past and immerse yourself in its ancient splendor.

Overview

The Kos Archaeological Museum is an exceptional repository of historical artifacts, spanning a vast timeline that encompasses the prehistoric, ancient Greek, and Roman periods. It is a place where the stories of the island come alive through meticulously curated exhibits.

Highlights

1. **Mosaics**: As you step into the museum, you'll be greeted by a mesmerizing display of intricately designed mosaics. These colorful and detailed mosaics often depict mythological scenes, offering a glimpse into the artistic and cultural achievements of the time.

2. **Statues and Sculptures**: The museum boasts an impressive collection of ancient statues and sculptures, with the most renowned being the statue of Hippocrates himself, the father of modern medicine. It's not just art; it's history brought to life.

3. **Pottery and Inscriptions**: For those intrigued by daily life in antiquity, the vast collection of pottery items and inscriptions is a treasure trove of information. These items reveal the practices,

customs, and language of the people who once inhabited the island.

Traveler Tips

- **Operating Hours:** The museum's operating hours may vary by season, so it's advisable to check in advance before planning your visit. However, it generally opens in the morning and closes in the evening.
- **Entrance Fee:** While there is an admission fee, it is a modest investment for the wealth of knowledge and historical insights you'll gain during your visit. Children and students often enjoy discounted rates.
- **Guided Tours:** Consider opting for a guided tour, which can provide you with a more in-depth and informative experience. Knowledgeable guides can explain the significance of each exhibit and help you navigate the museum's extensive collection.
- **Combine with Other Attractions:** The Kos Archaeological Museum is conveniently located in Kos Town, close to other historical sites, including the Casa Romana. Combining your visit with nearby attractions allows you to make the most of your time and experience the island's history holistically.
- **Photography:** Photography is allowed in most areas of the museum. Capture memories of the

captivating artifacts, but be mindful of other visitors and the museum's regulations.

The Kos Archaeological Museum is more than just a collection of ancient relics; it's a journey through time. It provides travelers with a unique opportunity to connect with the island's history, appreciate its cultural significance, and deepen their understanding of the people who once called Kos their home. Don't miss the chance to explore this remarkable museum during your visit to Kos.

Casa Romana (Roman House)

Casa Romana, also known as the Roman House, is a remarkable archaeological site located in the heart of Kos Town, on the beautiful island of Kos in Greece. This well-preserved Roman villa is a testament to the island's rich history, providing visitors with a unique opportunity to step back in time and explore the daily life and opulence of ancient Roman residents. Casa Romana is a captivating historical site that offers an immersive journey into the past, making it a must-visit destination for history enthusiasts and cultural explorers.

History and Significance

Casa Romana dates back to the 2nd century AD when the Romans ruled over Kos. This elegant villa, adorned with intricate mosaics, frescoes, and architectural marvels, is a prime example of Roman domestic architecture during this era. It was likely the residence of a wealthy Roman citizen or a high-ranking official.

The villa's historical significance lies not only in its architecture but also in the insights it provides into the daily life, social customs, and artistic preferences of the Roman elite on the island of Kos. Exploring Casa Romana is like uncovering a time capsule, where visitors can marvel at the ancient artistry and craftsmanship of a bygone era.

Key Features

1. Mosaics and Frescoes

The most striking aspect of Casa Romana is its beautifully preserved mosaics and frescoes. These intricate floor mosaics and wall paintings are not only aesthetically pleasing but also provide glimpses into the artistic tastes and cultural influences of the time. Scenes from Greek mythology, geometric patterns, and detailed depictions of flora and fauna adorn the villa's floors and walls.

2. Courtyard and Atrium

Casa Romana features a central courtyard and atrium, which were pivotal to the layout of Roman homes. The atrium served as the main living space, often containing a shallow pool (impluvium) to collect rainwater. Visitors can admire the architecture of the atrium and its function in collecting and preserving water.

3. Archaeological Insights

The ongoing archaeological excavations and restoration efforts at Casa Romana provide an opportunity for visitors to witness the preservation process and gain a deeper understanding of how historical sites are maintained and presented.

Traveler Tips

- **Operating Hours:** Casa Romana typically maintains consistent opening hours, making it easier to plan your visit. However, it's advisable to check in advance as there may be seasonal variations.

- **Admission Fee:** There is an admission fee to enter Casa Romana, but it's well worth the cost for the historical and cultural insights it offers.

- **Audio Guide:** The site offers informative audio guides in multiple languages, enhancing your understanding of the villa's history and features.

Combining with Other Attractions

Casa Romana is conveniently located in Kos Town, making it easy to combine your visit with other nearby attractions, such as the Archaeological Museum, the Hippocrates Tree, and the historical streets of the town.

Exploring these attractions in tandem allows you to delve deeper into the island's rich history and culture.

Overall, Casa Romana stands as a testament to the island's enduring legacy, preserving the art and architecture of ancient Roman civilization.

Hippocrates Tree

Location: Kos Town

The Hippocrates Tree in Kos Town is a living symbol of ancient history and an essential stop for travelers seeking to connect with the island's rich cultural and medical heritage. According to legend, this venerable plane tree is a direct descendant of the original tree planted by Hippocrates, the Father of Medicine, around 500 BC. This remarkable living relic stands as a testament to the enduring legacy of the island of Kos.

Historical Significance: The Hippocrates Tree holds immense historical and cultural significance, primarily attributed to the following:

1. **Hippocratic Oath:** Hippocrates, the ancient Greek physician, is renowned for his groundbreaking contributions to medicine. The Hippocratic Oath, a foundational ethical code for medical practitioners, is named after him. It reflects principles of medical

ethics and professionalism and is still relevant in the field of healthcare today.

2. **Father of Medicine:** Hippocrates' groundbreaking work in medicine laid the foundation for modern medical practice. He emphasized the importance of observation, clinical examination, and treating the patient as a whole.

3. **Legendary Planting:** The legend of Hippocrates planting the original tree speaks to his connection with the healing arts. The shade of the tree is believed to have provided a peaceful setting for him to teach his students about medicine and philosophy.

Traveler Tips:

- **Free Entry:** Visiting the Hippocrates Tree is free of charge, making it accessible to all travelers.

- **Reflective Atmosphere:** The site exudes a serene and reflective atmosphere, allowing visitors to appreciate the historical significance and ponder the legacy of Hippocrates.

- **Nearby Attractions:** The tree is conveniently located near the Castle of the Knights and other historical landmarks in Kos Town, making it an excellent addition to a broader exploration of the island's history.

Visiting the Hippocrates Tree is not only a chance to witness a remarkable living relic but also an opportunity to pay homage to the ancient physician whose influence continues to shape the field of medicine.

Family-Friendly Activities

Kos is not just a paradise for adults; it's also a fantastic destination for families. This chapter highlights some of the best family-friendly activities and experiences that will make your visit to Kos memorable for all members of the family.

Hippocrates Garden Cultural Center

Description: The Hippocrates Garden Cultural Center is a hidden gem on the island of Kos, Greece. Named after the ancient Greek physician Hippocrates, this center offers a unique and immersive experience for travelers of all ages, making it a perfect destination for families looking to explore the island's rich history and culture.

What to Expect

1. Educational Workshops

One of the highlights of the Hippocrates Garden Cultural Center is its engaging and informative workshops. These workshops delve into the fascinating world of ancient Greek medicine and philosophy. Led by knowledgeable guides, you and your family can learn about the practices and beliefs that laid the foundation for modern medicine. Through interactive sessions, you'll gain a deeper understanding of the principles that Hippocrates and other ancient scholars developed.

2. Herb Garden Exploration

The center boasts a lush and beautifully maintained herb garden that's both educational and visually captivating. Take a leisurely stroll through the garden and discover various herbs and plants, some of which have medicinal properties. Your family can learn about the traditional uses of these plants, which played a crucial role in ancient Greek medicine. It's a sensory experience that engages visitors of all ages.

3. Mythology and Ancient Greece

Intriguing storytelling and exhibits at the Hippocrates Garden Cultural Center transport you back to the world of ancient Greece. Uncover the myths and legends that shaped Greek culture and explore the historical context of the time. This immersive approach helps children and adults alike connect with the island's rich cultural heritage.

4. Hands-On Activities

The center's hands-on activities are perfect for families. Whether it's replicating ancient medical procedures or engaging in fun and interactive displays, these activities make learning a dynamic and enjoyable experience. It's an excellent way to keep children entertained while providing a deeper appreciation of the island's history.

5. Café and Gift Shop

After your exploration, take a break at the on-site café where you can savor traditional Greek cuisine or enjoy a cup of coffee. The café offers a relaxing atmosphere for the whole family. Don't forget to stop by the gift shop, where you can find unique souvenirs and educational materials related to the center's themes.

Why Families Love It

The Hippocrates Garden Cultural Center offers a departure from the usual tourist attractions, providing an engaging and educational experience that the whole family can enjoy. It offers a wonderful opportunity to introduce children to the captivating world of ancient Greece, medicine, and philosophy. Moreover, the center's welcoming and knowledgeable staff make it a warm and family-friendly destination, ensuring that your visit is both enriching and enjoyable.

Visiting the Hippocrates Garden Cultural Center is not only an opportunity to learn about the past but also a chance to create lasting memories with your family on the beautiful island of Kos. It's a unique and enriching experience that adds depth to your travel adventures and leaves you with a better understanding of the island's heritage.

Lido Water Park

Description: If you're traveling to Kos with your family, you won't want to miss the Lido Water Park. Situated on the eastern coast of the island, this aquatic wonderland is designed to deliver a day of fun and excitement for visitors of all ages. Whether you're seeking thrilling water adventures or simply want to relax by the pool, Lido Water Park has something for everyone.

What to Expect:

- **Water Slides and Attractions**: The main attraction at Lido Water Park is, of course, the impressive array of water slides and attractions. These slides cater to all age groups and levels of adventure, ensuring there's something for every member of the family. From gentle, meandering slides perfect for little ones to high-speed thrill rides that will get the adrenaline pumping for older kids and adults, the options are extensive.

- **Lazy River**: For a more leisurely experience, don't miss the Lazy River. This slow-moving, meandering water course is perfect for relaxation.

Grab an inflatable tube, lay back, and let the gentle current carry you along. It's an excellent way to unwind while enjoying the beautiful surroundings.

- **Kid-Friendly Pools**: Lido Water Park doesn't overlook the littlest members of the family. There are dedicated pools for younger children, with shallower waters and splash zones that ensure their safety and endless entertainment.

- **Sunbathing and Relaxation**: While the kids splash around and explore, parents can unwind in the sun. There are plenty of lounging areas equipped with sunbeds, allowing you to soak up the Mediterranean sun while keeping a watchful eye on your children.

- **Cafes and Snack Bars**: When it's time for a break, you won't need to venture far. Lido Water Park features cafes and snack bars where you can grab refreshments, light meals, and snacks throughout the day.

Why Families Love It: What sets Lido Water Park apart is its ability to cater to the entire family. It's not just about the water slides and rides; it's also about the safe, clean, and family-friendly environment. Lifeguards are always on duty, ensuring everyone's safety and peace of mind. This water park is a great place for families to bond, make memories, and experience the thrill of aquatic adventures in a beautiful setting.

Nightlife and Entertainment in Kos

Kos doesn't only enchant visitors with its natural beauty and historical sites; it also offers a vibrant and diverse nightlife scene. From beachfront bars to dance clubs, there's something for every night owl. Here's your comprehensive guide to the nightlife and entertainment options in Kos.

Kos Town Nightlife

Kos Town, the capital of the island, is where you'll find the most bustling nightlife on Kos. Here's a more detailed look at what to expect when exploring the nightlife options in the town:

- **Bars and Pubs**: Kos Town boasts an impressive selection of bars and pubs. These establishments vary from cozy, family-run tavernas to modern cocktail bars. Whether you're seeking a relaxed atmosphere or a trendy place to kick off your night, you'll find it here. **Makrigiannis Street** and **Diakon** streets are popular bar-hopping areas.

- **Dance Clubs**: As the evening progresses, the dance clubs in Kos Town come to life. Expect to find a diverse range of music styles, from the latest international hits to classic Greek tracks. Popular venues include **Cavo Paradiso** and **Heaven Club**. The nightlife in these clubs often continues well past midnight, making them great spots for night owls.

- **Live Music**: If you're more inclined towards live music, there are numerous venues in Kos Town featuring local bands and solo artists. You can catch performances spanning various genres, including Greek folk music, jazz, and rock. The atmosphere in these venues is usually more intimate, perfect for a relaxed night out.

- **Beachfront Parties**: Some of the beach bars and clubs in Kos Town throw unique parties right on the shoreline. Imagine dancing under the starlit Greek sky with your feet in the sand, or lounging by the water, sipping a cocktail while listening to music from renowned DJs. These beachfront parties offer a perfect combination of relaxation and nightlife excitement.

- **Themed Nights**: Kos Town often hosts themed nights, and these can be a highlight of your visit. One such theme is the Greek night, where you can enjoy traditional Greek music and dance performances. These evenings provide a wonderful opportunity to immerse yourself in the island's culture and even try your hand (or feet) at Greek dance.

Traditional Greek Evenings

For those interested in experiencing the essence of Greek culture and entertainment in a lively and engaging setting, Traditional Greek Evenings are an excellent choice. Here's a deeper look into what these evenings entail:

- **Live Music**: Live Greek music is a central element of Traditional Greek Evenings. It typically features traditional instruments like the bouzouki, an instrument central to Greek music. The musicians not only entertain but also encourage guests to participate, either by singing along or dancing to the music.

- **Greek Dancing**: Professional dancers take the stage, performing traditional Greek dances like the sirtaki, made famous in the movie "Zorba the Greek," and the zeibekiko, a passionate and improvisational dance. Often, audience members are invited to join the dancers on the floor and try out these joyful and expressive dances.

- **Greek Cuisine**: Traditional Greek evenings are culinary feasts. You can savor a variety of Greek dishes, including moussaka, a layered eggplant and meat casserole, and souvlaki, skewered and grilled meat served with pita and tzatziki. To sweeten the deal, you'll be treated to Greek desserts like

[112]

baklava, a pastry with layers of nuts and honey. Pair your meal with local wine or perhaps try the anise-flavored aperitif, ouzo.

These evenings provide more than just entertainment; they offer a profound cultural experience. You'll leave with a deeper appreciation for Greek traditions and the warmth of the island's people.

Safety and Tips

- **Drink Responsibly**: While the nightlife in Kos is undoubtedly enjoyable, always remember to consume alcohol responsibly. Know your limits, and ensure you have a safe way to get back to your accommodation. Walking or using local transportation is often safer than driving, especially if you're planning to enjoy a drink or two.

- **Dress Code**: Many clubs and upscale bars in Kos Town have dress codes, so it's advisable to dress neatly and presentably. However, some beach bars and more casual venues may have a more relaxed dress code, especially during the summer months.

- **Local Events**: Keep an eye on local event listings and festivals that may coincide with your visit. Kos regularly hosts cultural and music festivals, providing additional entertainment options and unique cultural experiences. Participating in these local events can be a fantastic way to connect with the local community.

- **Reservations**: If you're planning to visit a specific nightclub, restaurant with entertainment, or a particularly popular venue, it's wise to make reservations, especially during the peak tourist season. This ensures you have a spot and avoids any disappointment due to overcrowding.

Kos's nightlife scene is diverse and dynamic, with options for party-goers, music lovers, and those looking to embrace Greek culture.

CHAPTER FIVE

CUISINE AND DINING

When it comes to experiencing the heart and soul of Kos, there's no better way than through its diverse and delectable cuisine. This chapter is your gateway to a culinary journey that will tantalize your taste buds and leave you craving more. From traditional Greek dishes to exquisite seafood, Kos offers a feast for all senses.

Traditional Greek Cuisine

Greek cuisine is a culinary journey that transcends time, combining fresh, wholesome ingredients with a rich history. When visiting Kos, you'll have the opportunity to savor traditional Greek dishes that have been perfected over generations. From hearty moussaka to the refreshing Greek salad, these classic dishes are a feast for the senses.

Moussaka

Moussaka is a beloved Greek dish, often considered the country's answer to lasagna. It's a hearty casserole with layers of flavor, including eggplant, minced meat (typically lamb or beef, but sometimes lentils for a vegetarian version), and a luscious béchamel sauce. Here's what you need to know about this Greek delight:

Ingredients:

- Eggplant: Sliced and often lightly fried before layering.

- Minced Meat: Usually lamb or beef, seasoned with herbs and spices.

- Potatoes: Some variations include thinly sliced potatoes for extra texture.

- Béchamel Sauce: A creamy sauce made with milk, butter, and eggs.

- Tomato Sauce: Adds a tangy and savory element to the dish.

Preparation:

1. Start by frying the sliced eggplant until it's lightly golden and set it aside.

2. Brown the minced meat and add spices like cinnamon and allspice.

3. Layer the eggplant, meat, and potatoes in a baking dish.

4. Pour a generous layer of tomato sauce over the top.

5. Finish with a creamy béchamel sauce.

6. Bake until the top is golden and the layers have melded together.

Serving: Moussaka is often served hot, with a crispy, golden top layer. It's a satisfying dish that pairs well with a fresh Greek salad and crusty bread.

Souvlaki

For a quick and satisfying street food experience in Kos, souvlaki is the way to go. These skewers of grilled and marinated meat (commonly pork or chicken) are served with pita bread, fresh vegetables, and a dollop of tzatziki sauce. Souvlaki is the epitome of Greek fast food, and here's what you need to know:

Ingredients:

- Meat: Pork or chicken, cut into small pieces.

- Marinade: A mixture of olive oil, lemon juice, garlic, and Greek herbs.

- Pita Bread: Soft, round flatbreads for wrapping.

- Tzatziki Sauce: A yogurt-based sauce with cucumbers, garlic, and dill.

- Fresh Vegetables: Typically, tomatoes, onions, and sometimes lettuce.

Preparation:

1. Marinate the meat in olive oil, lemon juice, garlic, and herbs.

2. Skewer the marinated meat and grill until charred and cooked through.

3. Warm the pita bread.

4. Assemble the souvlaki by placing the grilled meat and fresh vegetables in the pita.

5. Drizzle with tzatziki sauce.

Serving: Souvlaki is often served in a pita wrap, making it a convenient and delicious on-the-go meal. It's a favorite for both locals and tourists and can be found in many street-side eateries throughout Kos.

Greek Salad (Horiatiki)

A Greek salad, or Horiatiki, is a vibrant and healthy dish that embodies the essence of Mediterranean cuisine. It's a refreshing mix of colorful vegetables and feta cheese, drizzled with olive oil and sprinkled with aromatic oregano. Here's what you need to know about this classic salad:

Ingredients:

- Tomatoes: Ripe and juicy, often cut into wedges.

- Cucumbers: Sliced or diced.

- Kalamata Olives: Dark, flavorful olives with a distinct taste.

- Red Onions: Thinly sliced for a mild kick.

- Feta Cheese: Creamy and tangy, often crumbled over the top.

- Green Peppers: Sliced or diced (optional).

- Olive Oil: Extra-virgin olive oil is used for dressing.

- Oregano: Adds a fragrant and earthy touch.

- Red Wine Vinegar: A splash for acidity.

- Salt and Pepper: Season to taste.

Preparation:

1. Toss together the tomatoes, cucumbers, olives, and onions in a bowl.

2. Crumble the feta cheese over the vegetables.

3. Drizzle with olive oil and red wine vinegar.

4. Sprinkle with oregano, salt, and pepper.

Serving: Greek salad is typically served as a side dish or as a starter. It's a perfect accompaniment to grilled meats or seafood. Enjoy it with a piece of crusty bread to soak up the flavorful juices.

Dolmades

Dolmades are a delightful Greek appetizer that consists of grape leaves stuffed with a flavorful mixture of rice, herbs, and sometimes ground meat. They are then simmered to perfection. Here's what you need to know about these savory bites:

Ingredients:

- Grape Leaves: Softened and blanched to make them pliable.

- Rice: Short-grain rice is commonly used.

- Fresh Herbs: Parsley, dill, and mint for a burst of flavor.

- Ground Meat (optional): Often, a small amount of minced meat is added.

- Onions: Finely chopped for aroma.

- Lemon Juice: Adds a zesty tang.

- Olive Oil: For a rich, Mediterranean flavor.

- Salt and Pepper: Season to taste.

Preparation:

1. Prepare the stuffing mixture by combining cooked rice, herbs, meat (if desired), onions, lemon juice, olive oil, salt, and pepper.

2. Place a grape leaf flat on a surface and add a spoonful of the stuffing in the center.

3. Fold the sides of the leaf over the filling, then roll it tightly.

4. Arrange the dolmades in a pot, seam-side down, and cover them with water and a drizzle of olive oil.

5. Simmer until the rice is tender and the flavors meld.

Serving: Dolmades are often served as a meze, or appetizer. They can be enjoyed warm or at room temperature, drizzled with a bit of lemon juice and olive oil.

Spanakopita

Spanakopita is a savory pastry that combines spinach, feta cheese, onions, and various herbs, all wrapped in flaky, golden-brown phyllo dough. It's a delightful dish that showcases the balance of flavors and textures in Greek cuisine. Here's what you need to know about this classic Greek pie:

Ingredients:

- Phyllo Dough: Thin, delicate pastry sheets.

- Spinach: Fresh spinach, cooked and drained.

- Feta Cheese: Crumbled and salty, it adds a rich flavor.

- Onions: Sautéed until soft and translucent.

- Fresh Herbs: Dill, parsley, and green onions for an aromatic touch.

- Eggs: Used as a binding agent.

- Olive Oil: For brushing the phyllo layers.

- Salt and Pepper: Season to taste.

Preparation:

1. Prepare the filling by mixing cooked spinach, crumbled feta cheese, sautéed onions, fresh herbs, eggs, olive oil, salt, and pepper.

2. Lay out one sheet of phyllo dough and brush it with olive oil. Place another sheet on top and repeat the process until you have a stack of several sheets.

3. Spread the spinach and feta filling evenly over the phyllo dough.

4. Fold the phyllo dough over the filling to create a neat package, and brush the top with more olive oil.

5. Bake until the pastry is golden and crisp.

Serving: Spanakopita can be served as an appetizer, side dish, or even as a light lunch. It's often cut into square or triangular portions and served warm, offering a delightful contrast between the crisp, flaky layers and the rich, savory filling.

Traditional Greek dishes like moussaka, souvlaki, Greek salad, dolmades, and spanakopita are just a glimpse into the delicious world of Greek cuisine. When visiting Kos, be sure to savor these dishes to experience the authentic flavors that have made Greek food beloved around the globe.

Seafood Delicacies

One of the highlights of visiting Kos is undoubtedly the abundance of fresh and flavorful seafood dishes. With its location in the heart of the Aegean Sea, the island boasts a wealth of seafood options that will leave seafood enthusiasts craving for more. Here, we explore some of the most delightful seafood delicacies that you simply must try when you're in Kos.

Fresh Catch of the Day

Kos's coastal waters offer a daily supply of the freshest catch, featuring a variety of delectable fish and shellfish. Fishermen bring in an assortment of treasures from the

Aegean Sea, and you can enjoy the catch of the day prepared in various mouthwatering ways.

What to Expect:

- Daily specials at local restaurants and tavernas.

- A chance to taste fish such as sea bream, sea bass, red mullet, and various types of shellfish.

- Fish often grilled, baked, or fried to perfection, seasoned with aromatic herbs and drizzled with quality olive oil.

- A rich, authentic maritime experience that brings the flavors of the sea to your plate.

Where to Try:

- Local tavernas and seafood restaurants near the coast.

- Ask your server for the freshest catch of the day, prepared in the chef's recommended style.

- Don't forget to pair your meal with a crisp local white wine or ouzo, a traditional Greek aperitif.

Grilled Calamari

Grilled calamari is a Mediterranean delicacy that combines the unique flavor of fresh squid with the simplicity of Greek cuisine. The tender and succulent calamari is marinated with olive oil, fragrant herbs, and a hint of lemon, then grilled to perfection.

What to Expect:

- A plate of perfectly grilled calamari served with a wedge of lemon.

- The squid is marinated with olive oil, garlic, oregano, and often a dash of red pepper flakes for a bit of heat.

- The smoky flavor from the grill complements the natural sweetness of the squid, creating a harmonious taste.

Where to Try:

- Most seafood restaurants in Kos offer grilled calamari on their menu.

- Look for beachside tavernas where you can savor this dish with a view of the sea.

Psarosoupa

For a taste of tradition and comfort, try Psarosoupa, a hearty Greek fish soup. Made with a variety of fish, fresh vegetables, and fragrant herbs, this dish warms the soul and delights the palate.

What to Expect:

- A flavorful, clear broth enriched with the essence of various fish, such as red snapper or grouper.

- Accompanied by vegetables like carrots, celery, onions, and aromatic herbs like dill and parsley.

- Served with a slice of lemon and fresh bread to soak up every delicious drop.

Where to Try:

- Psarosoupa is often found on the menus of traditional Greek tavernas.

- It's an ideal choice for those seeking a comforting, nutritious, and authentic Greek meal.

Garides Saganaki

Garides Saganaki is a savory Greek dish that spotlights succulent shrimp cooked in a delightful tomato and feta cheese sauce. Seasoned with fragrant herbs and spices, it's baked until bubbly and golden, offering a symphony of flavors that will leave you craving more.

What to Expect:

- Jumbo shrimp bathed in a rich tomato sauce, featuring garlic, onions, bell peppers, and a sprinkle of fresh herbs.

- Generously topped with crumbled feta cheese for a creamy and tangy finish.

- Baked until the shrimp are tender and the cheese is slightly browned and bubbling.

Where to Try:

- Many seafood restaurants in Kos offer Garides Saganaki.

- It's a fantastic dish to share, especially when paired with crusty bread to soak up the scrumptious sauce.

Kos's seafood delicacies are a testament to the island's rich maritime heritage and the bounty of the Aegean Sea. Exploring these dishes is not only a culinary adventure but also a celebration of the island's culture and traditions. Seafood enthusiasts, don't miss the opportunity to savor these delectable dishes when you visit Kos!

Dining Etiquette

Dining etiquette is an essential aspect of experiencing the local culture when visiting Kos, Greece. Understanding and respecting the dining customs can enhance your dining experience and leave a positive impression on the locals. Here, we'll delve into the key dining etiquette tips to ensure a smooth and respectful dining experience.

Tipping

Tipping is customary in Kos and is a way to show your appreciation for good service. Here are some tips on tipping etiquette:

- **Restaurants**: In restaurants, it is customary to leave a tip of around 10% to 15% of the total bill. Many restaurants include a service charge in the bill, but it's still a common practice to leave a small additional tip for exceptional service.

- **Cafés**: In cafés, it's common to round up your bill or leave some small change as a tip.

- **Taxi Drivers**: Tipping taxi drivers is also customary. You can round up the fare or leave a small tip as a gesture of appreciation.

- **Tour Guides**: When taking tours or excursions, consider tipping your tour guide if they provide an informative and enjoyable experience. The amount can vary, but 5-10% of the tour cost is a common guideline.

Dress Code

The dress code for dining in Kos varies depending on the type of restaurant. Here are some general guidelines:

- **Casual Dining**: For most casual and beachfront restaurants, casual attire is acceptable. You can wear comfortable clothing, including beachwear like shorts and flip-flops. However, it's advisable to cover up when you're not on the beach.

- **Smart-Casual Dining**: For more upscale or fine dining restaurants, a smart-casual dress code is often in place. Men may be expected to wear collared shirts, long pants, and closed-toe shoes, while women may wear dresses, skirts, or smart-casual attire.

- **Beachfront Eateries**: Many beachfront restaurants are lenient when it comes to attire, and beachwear is generally acceptable. However, it's respectful to cover up when you're not on the beach or to check with the establishment about their dress code.

Meal Times

Greek meal times may differ from what you're accustomed to in other countries. Here are some important notes on meal times in Kos:

- **Lunch**: Greeks typically have lunch later in the day, around 2:00 PM. Many local businesses and shops close for a few hours during this time, allowing people to enjoy a leisurely meal.

- **Dinner**: Dinner is often enjoyed late, around 9:00 PM. This is the time when restaurants and tavernas come to life, and it's a great opportunity to savor the local cuisine.

- **Tourist-Friendly Places**: In areas popular with tourists, dining hours are often more flexible. You can usually find restaurants and eateries that offer meals at various times to accommodate different schedules.

Kos's Best Restaurants

Here are some of the island's best restaurants, each offering a unique dining experience that perfectly complements the island's beauty.

Taverna Ta Pitsounakia

Location: Agios Theologos, Kos

Cuisine: Authentic Greek

Description: Nestled in the quaint village of Agios Theologos, Taverna Ta Pitsounakia is a family-owned gem. This charming taverna is renowned for its authentic Greek cuisine, served in a rustic and welcoming atmosphere. The highlight of the menu is the succulent lamb dishes, slow-cooked to perfection, and seasoned with fragrant herbs. Make sure to leave room for dessert, as their homemade baklava is a delightful way to end your meal.

Petrino

Location: Agios Fokas,

Cuisine: Mediterranean Fusion

Description: Located in Agios Fokas, Petrino is a culinary gem that seamlessly blends Mediterranean and international flavors. The restaurant boasts a spectacular view of the Aegean Sea and offers a modern, elegant dining experience. The menu is a creative fusion of fresh seafood and local ingredients, prepared with a contemporary twist. Petrino is the perfect place for a special evening, with exquisite dishes and impeccable service.

Kardamena Fish Restaurant

Location: Kardamena, Kos

Cuisine: Fresh Seafood

Description: If you're seeking a laid-back dining experience with a focus on fresh seafood, the Kardamena Fish Restaurant is your destination. Situated in the picturesque village of Kardamena, this restaurant offers a casual yet delightful atmosphere. The menu features a variety of fish and seafood delicacies, prepared with a simplicity that allows the ingredients' natural flavors to shine. Pair your meal with a local wine for an authentic Greek dining experience.

Mavromatis

Location: Kos Town

Cuisine: Greek and International

Description: For those seeking an elegant dining experience in the heart of Kos Town, Mavromatis is the place to be. This upscale restaurant offers an extensive menu that combines traditional Greek dishes with international flavors. The stylish and sophisticated setting is perfect for a special evening out. Whether you're in the mood for fresh seafood or savory grilled meats, Mavromatis caters to a variety of tastes.

Sunset Taverna

Location: Agios Stefanos

Cuisine: Traditional Greek

Description: As the name suggests, Sunset Taverna is the perfect spot to enjoy breathtaking sunset views over the sea. This family-run taverna offers a relaxed and welcoming atmosphere, making it an ideal choice for families and couples alike. The menu features a wide array of Greek classics, including grilled meats, fresh seafood, and an impressive selection of meze. The combination of delicious food and a stunning view creates a memorable dining experience.

These restaurants represent just a glimpse of the culinary treasures waiting for you on the island of Kos. Whether you're craving authentic Greek flavors or innovative fusion cuisine, Kos's dining scene has something to satisfy every palate. Don't miss the opportunity to savor the delicious offerings of these establishments during your visit to this Greek paradise.

CHAPTER SIX

OUTDOOR ADVENTURES

Kos is not just a place for sunbathing and sipping cocktails by the beach; it's a paradise for outdoor enthusiasts. From crystal-clear waters to scenic hiking trails, this chapter explores the plethora of outdoor adventures waiting for you on this beautiful Greek island.

Beaches and Watersports

Kos boasts some of the most beautiful beaches in the Mediterranean. From idyllic, sandy shores to thrilling watersports, this section is your gateway to the ultimate beach and water adventure in Kos.

Kardamena Beach

Nestled along the southern coast of Kos, Kardamena Beach is a vibrant and bustling coastal gem that attracts travelers from all corners of the world. Known as the "Windsurfing Capital of Kos," this beach is a haven for water sports enthusiasts and sun-seekers alike. Let's dive deeper into what makes Kardamena Beach so special.

Beach Paradise

Kardamena Beach is a pristine, golden sandy expanse that stretches for nearly three kilometers, making it one of the most extensive and attractive beaches on the island. The soft sand here is perfect for lounging, building sandcastles, or practicing yoga with the soothing sound of the waves as your backdrop. With plenty of sunbeds and umbrellas available for rent, you can comfortably relax under the warm Greek sun.

Watersports Extravaganza

The highlight of Kardamena Beach is undoubtedly the plethora of watersports activities on offer. Thanks to its consistent winds, Kardamena has earned a reputation as a windsurfing and kiteboarding paradise. Here's a closer look at the aquatic adventures you can embark on:

Windsurfing: Kardamena's brisk and reliable winds create an ideal environment for windsurfing. Whether you're a seasoned windsurfer or a novice looking to learn, local windsurfing schools and rental shops are ready to assist. Expert instructors can guide you through the basics, and advanced surfers will find the conditions perfect for exciting rides.

Kiteboarding: Kiteboarding, a thrilling water sport that combines elements of surfing and wakeboarding, is a big draw on Kardamena Beach. The steady winds and shallow waters make it an excellent spot for beginners and experienced kiteboarders alike. Lessons, equipment rentals, and experienced guides are readily available.

Jet Skiing: For those seeking an adrenaline rush, jet skiing is a must-try activity. Rent a jet ski and zip across the waves, feeling the sea spray on your face as you explore the coastline.

Beachfront Ambiance

Beyond the watersports action, Kardamena Beach offers a lively beachfront scene with an array of beach bars, restaurants, and shops. Enjoy a cold beverage and some delicious Greek cuisine at one of the many beachside tavernas. As the day turns to night, Kardamena's nightlife comes alive, with beach parties and music filling the air.

Windsurfing Competitions

Kardamena Beach hosts windsurfing competitions throughout the year, attracting athletes and spectators from around the world. These events provide a unique opportunity to witness the skill and grace of windsurfing pros while enjoying the stunning backdrop of the Aegean Sea.

Overall, Kardamena Beach is a vibrant, action-packed destination that caters to water sports enthusiasts, beach lovers, and those in search of lively entertainment.

Mastichari Beach

Nestled on the western coast of Kos, Mastichari Beach is a hidden gem that beckons travelers in search of serenity and water adventures. This pristine stretch of shoreline is distinguished by its calm, crystal-clear waters and a tranquil atmosphere, making it an excellent destination for those seeking a more relaxed and nature-oriented beach experience.

Beach Beauty and Landscape

Mastichari Beach's beauty lies in its simplicity. It boasts fine, soft sands that extend along the shoreline, creating an inviting carpet for beachgoers to lay their towels on. The beach's azure waters are so transparent that you can see the ocean floor, making it an idyllic spot for swimming, wading, or just floating in the gentle, shallow waters.

The beach is also framed by a backdrop of dunes and greenery, providing natural shade for those who prefer to escape the sun's rays during the hottest hours of the day. The absence of bustling crowds adds to the tranquil ambiance, making it the perfect spot to unwind and recharge.

Watersports and Activities

Mastichari Beach is renowned for its exceptional watersports and underwater activities. Whether you're an experienced diver or someone just dipping their toes into the world of snorkeling, this beach caters to all levels of water enthusiasts.

1. Snorkeling: The clarity of the water at Mastichari Beach is truly remarkable, making it an ideal location for snorkeling. Don your mask and fins, and you'll discover a captivating underwater world filled with vibrant marine life, underwater caves, and intriguing rock formations. Many local dive shops offer snorkeling gear for rent and guided excursions to the best underwater spots.

2. Scuba Diving: For those looking to delve even deeper into the underwater realm, Mastichari Beach is a gateway to a world of scuba diving adventures. Experienced divers will find a variety of dive sites within easy reach, including underwater shipwrecks and mesmerizing geological formations. If you're new to scuba diving, local dive operators offer training and certification courses to get you started.

Dining and Amenities

Mastichari village, situated just a short walk from the beach, is home to a selection of charming tavernas and beachfront restaurants. After a day of aquatic exploration, you can savor fresh seafood and traditional Greek dishes while relishing the peaceful coastal views. Whether it's a leisurely seafood feast or a simple coffee by the sea, the local culinary scene complements the relaxed atmosphere of Mastichari Beach perfectly.

Practical Tips

- **Sun Protection**: While enjoying the peaceful beach, ensure you have ample sun protection. Sunscreen, a wide-brimmed hat, and sunglasses are your best friends.

- **Snorkeling Gear**: If you're planning to snorkel, it's advisable to rent or bring your snorkeling gear. Many beachfront vendors offer gear rentals, but having your equipment ensures a comfortable and more personalized experience.

- **Dining**: Explore the charming village of Mastichari for authentic Greek dining experiences. Try fresh seafood dishes and don't miss out on the local specialties.

Mastichari Beach is not only a tranquil seaside haven but also a gateway to the mesmerizing underwater world of the Aegean Sea. Whether you're looking to explore the rich marine life or simply unwind on the serene sands, Mastichari Beach is an essential stop on your Kos adventure.

Agios Stefanos Beach

Agios Stefanos Beach is situated at the southernmost tip of Kos, overlooking the tranquil waters of the Aegean Sea. It's a place where the pristine shoreline meets the rocky cliffs, creating a captivating contrast of nature's elements. The area is characterized by its rugged coastline, crystal-clear waters, and a gentle sea breeze that adds to the overall sense of tranquility.

Activities and Watersports

The beach, although quieter than some of Kos's more popular destinations, offers a range of activities for those who seek adventure or relaxation:

Paddleboarding: Rent a paddleboard and leisurely explore the calm waters surrounding Agios Stefanos. The tranquil sea is perfect for paddleboarding, allowing you to soak in the natural beauty at your own pace.

Kayaking: Similar to paddleboarding, kayaking is a great way to enjoy the serene environment of Agios Stefanos Beach. Paddle along the coast, admiring the picturesque cliffs and clear waters.

Swimming: The gently sloping beach and calm sea make it an ideal spot for swimming. The waters are so clear that you can often see the sea floor, and the temperature is comfortably warm during the summer months.

Relaxation: If you prefer simply lazing in the sun, Agios Stefanos Beach is perfect for that too. Lay out your beach towel or rent a sunbed, and enjoy the peaceful surroundings.

Local Charm

Agios Stefanos is more than just a beach; it's a glimpse into the authentic side of Kos. The small village of

Kefalos nearby adds to the area's charm, with traditional Greek architecture and a friendly local community. You'll find quaint tavernas and cafes where you can savor local dishes and refreshments.

Natural Beauty

The dramatic cliffs and the lush vegetation that surrounds Agios Stefanos Beach contribute to its captivating beauty. Hiking enthusiasts will find nearby trails leading to elevated viewpoints offering breathtaking vistas of the sea and the surrounding landscape.

Sunset Magic

One of the most enchanting aspects of Agios Stefanos Beach is the incredible sunset views. As the day comes to a close, the setting sun casts a warm, golden glow on the sea, creating a picture-perfect moment that's both serene and romantic.

In a world that's often bustling and fast-paced, Agios Stefanos Beach stands as a reminder of the natural beauty and tranquility that Greece's islands can offer.

Paradise Beach
Location: Kefalos, Southern Kos

Paradise Beach is aptly named, offering a slice of heaven with its fine white sand and emerald waters. This popular spot combines relaxation with watersports activities:

Banana Boat Rides: Gather your friends and hop on a banana boat for an exciting, bumpy ride that guarantees laughter and splashes.

Parasailing: Get a bird's-eye view of Paradise Beach by parasailing. Soar above the sea while safely harnessed to a parachute.

Beach Volleyball: Many beachfront bars and clubs have beach volleyball courts where you can join a game or start your own.

Tigaki Beach
Location: Tigaki, Northern Kos

Tigaki Beach is known for its long stretches of soft sand and shallow, calm waters. It's a haven for families and water sports enthusiasts alike:

Windsurfing: The mild winds make Tigaki perfect for windsurfing beginners. Lessons are available for those looking to try this sport for the first time.

Pedal Boating: Rent a pedal boat to explore the coastline, enjoying a leisurely workout on the water while taking in the picturesque surroundings.

Kite Flying: Tigaki's consistent breezes make it an excellent spot for kite flying. You can purchase kites locally or bring your own.

Psalidi Beach

Location: Psalidi, Eastern Kos

Psalidi Beach offers a mix of relaxation and activities within close reach of Kos Town. What you can enjoy here:

Canoeing: Rent a canoe and explore the shoreline at your own pace, taking in the tranquil atmosphere and the scenery.

Yoga and Meditation: Some parts of Psalidi Beach offer a peaceful ambiance, ideal for yoga and meditation. Local instructors may offer classes on the beach.

Scenic Walks: Stroll along the coastline, breathing in the fresh sea air while enjoying views of the Turkish coast in the distance.

Remember to respect the local environment and adhere to safety guidelines while enjoying the beaches and watersports in Kos. Many beachside clubs and rental shops offer equipment and lessons, making it easy for both beginners and experienced adventurers to have an incredible time by the sea. Kos's diverse beaches and watersports activities ensure that you can choose your preferred level of action and relaxation, creating lasting memories on this magnificent island.

Hiking and Nature Trails

Kos, with its diverse and breathtaking natural landscapes, is a paradise for hikers and nature enthusiasts. This section will guide you through the island's most captivating hiking and nature trails, promising you an unforgettable adventure in the heart of the Greek Aegean.

Mount Dikeos

Mount Dikeos, the crown jewel of Kos, stands as the tallest peak on the island, towering majestically at 846 meters (2,776 feet) above sea level. This imposing mountain, whose name is derived from the Greek word for justice (dikaios), embodies the ancient myths and natural beauty that are synonymous with the Aegean landscape. Hiking Mount Dikeos is an experience that combines physical challenge with spiritual awakening as you traverse its ancient paths and bask in the unrivaled panoramic views of the island and the surrounding sea.

Trail Highlights

The Asclepius Cave: The Asclepius Cave is an essential stop on the Mount Dikeos hike. This cave is not only a sanctuary dedicated to the ancient god of medicine, Asclepius, but also a natural marvel. Its cool, damp interior and intriguing rock formations offer a sense of reverence and connection to the island's ancient past.

360-Degree Views: As you ascend Mount Dikeos, the journey is punctuated by breathtaking views that gradually reveal themselves. From the summit, you're rewarded with a 360-degree panorama of the Aegean Sea, the nearby islands, and the rugged, undulating terrain of Kos itself. The awe-inspiring beauty of the Aegean stretches before you, making the challenging ascent entirely worthwhile.

Varied Flora and Fauna: The hike takes you through diverse landscapes, from rocky paths to lush forests and stretches of arid land. As you navigate this ecological tapestry, keep an eye out for the island's unique wildlife, including the charming Hermann's tortoise. Birdwatchers will also appreciate the opportunity to spot various avian species, adding to the island's natural allure.

Ancient Ruins: The hike is punctuated with the remnants of ancient settlements, adding a historical layer to your adventure. These evocative ruins whisper tales of civilizations that once thrived on the island, creating a sense of awe and wonder as you explore this living tapestry of time.

Trail Difficulty

The Mount Dikeos hike is, in essence, a moderate to challenging endeavor. The terrain can be steep, rocky, and uneven, requiring proper hiking boots and a fair degree of physical fitness. Given the island's warm climate, be sure to carry an ample supply of water, especially on hot days. It's also advisable to take breaks as needed to rest and soak in the extraordinary vistas.

The ascent of Mount Dikeos is not just a physical journey; it's a spiritual and historical one as well. To truly appreciate the marvels of this mountain, consider embarking on the hike with a knowledgeable guide who can provide insight into the geological, cultural, and historical significance of this remarkable place.

Conquering Mount Dikeos is not just about reaching its summit; it's about immersing yourself in the mythology, history, and natural beauty of Kos. The summit provides an unrivaled vantage point from which to appreciate the enchanting island you've chosen to explore. Enjoy your adventure to the fullest and cherish the memories of Mount Dikeos for years to come.

Zia Village

Nestled on the slopes of Mount Dikeos, Zia Village is a picturesque gem that should not be missed by any traveler seeking a tranquil and authentic Greek experience. This charming village is renowned not only for its stunning sunset views but also for its enchanting hiking and nature trails, making it a hiker's paradise on the island of Kos.

Embracing the Sunset Magic

Zia is most famous for its spectacular sunsets. Visitors flock to this idyllic village to witness the sun slowly dip below the horizon, casting hues of orange, pink, and purple across the Aegean Sea. The views from Zia are nothing short of magical, making it the perfect destination for a romantic evening or a peaceful retreat. The easy hike to the viewpoint is both rewarding and accessible, ensuring that you won't miss this natural wonder.

Exploring Traditional Greek Villages

As you traverse the hiking trails around Zia, you'll find yourself wandering through traditional Greek villages that have retained their authenticity over the years. Whitewashed houses with blue accents, cobblestone streets, and the sweet scent of Mediterranean flora greet you at every turn. These villages offer a glimpse into the traditional way of life on the island, where time seems to stand still.

In these villages, you can interact with the locals, experience their warm hospitality, and savor traditional Greek cuisine in cozy tavernas. The aroma of freshly baked bread, the sounds of laughter in the village square, and the simple joys of life provide a unique and heartwarming experience for hikers.

Nature Photography and Wildlife

The landscape surrounding Zia is a paradise for nature photographers and wildlife enthusiasts. The trails through the hills and valleys of Mount Dikeos are adorned with a rich tapestry of flora, making it an ideal location for capturing the essence of nature. You can photograph the vibrant wildflowers, aromatic herbs, and striking rock formations that define the region.

Nature enthusiasts will also appreciate the diverse wildlife that calls this area home. From the graceful flight of butterflies to the mesmerizing chirping of cicadas, Zia's natural beauty is a sensory delight. If you're fortunate, you may spot small mammals or even the Hermann's tortoise, a unique species native to the region.

Trail Difficulty

Most of the hiking trails around Zia are of moderate difficulty, catering to hikers with varying experience levels. These paths are well-marked and maintained, ensuring a comfortable and safe hiking experience. While the terrain can be uneven at times, wearing suitable hiking footwear will make your journey more enjoyable.

Plaka Forest

Plaka Forest is a hidden gem on the island of Kos, offering a serene escape from the bustling beaches and vibrant towns. This enchanting forest, located near the village of Antimachia in the southwestern part of the island, is a haven for nature enthusiasts and those seeking a peaceful retreat. In this section, we'll delve deeper into what makes Plaka Forest a unique and rejuvenating experience.

Overview

Plaka Forest is a refreshing contrast to the typical coastal landscapes of Kos. As you enter the forest, you'll be greeted by a dense canopy of towering pine, cypress, and oak trees. The forest is a testament to the island's diverse ecology, providing an opportunity to explore lush greenery and enjoy a cooler climate, especially during the hot summer months.

Trail Highlights

Shaded Walks

One of the most alluring features of Plaka Forest is the canopy of trees that offers welcome shade during your walks. The well-maintained walking paths wind through the forest, providing you with a cool and tranquil environment in which to explore. These paths are perfect for leisurely strolls, contemplative walks, or even short hikes.

Birdwatching

Plaka Forest is a paradise for birdwatchers. The diverse vegetation and abundant birdlife make it an ideal location for spotting various bird species. Be sure to bring your binoculars and a bird guide to identify the birds that call this forest home.

Picnic Spots

The forest has designated picnic areas where you can relax and savor a meal amidst nature. Whether you're enjoying a picnic with family and friends or seeking a solitary escape, these spots provide a perfect setting for a memorable outdoor dining experience.

Mountain Biking

For those with a passion for mountain biking, Plaka Forest offers a network of trails suitable for cycling. The undulating terrain and natural obstacles provide an exciting and challenging course for bikers of all levels. Feel the rush of wind as you navigate through the forest's paths and enjoy the thrill of off-road biking.

Trail Difficulty

The trails within Plaka Forest cater to a wide range of fitness levels and preferences. From easy, level paths perfect for a family outing to more challenging terrain for seasoned hikers, the forest has something to offer everyone. The difficulty of the trails varies, so you can choose the one that best suits your hiking or walking abilities.

Tips for Exploring Plaka Forest

- **Prepare Adequately**: Ensure you're well-prepared for your visit to Plaka Forest. This includes bringing sufficient water, comfortable walking shoes, and appropriate clothing for the season.

- **Respect Nature**: As you explore the forest, remember to respect the environment. Avoid littering, and do not disturb the local wildlife. This will help maintain the natural beauty of the forest for future generations.

- **Check Local Regulations**: Before your visit, it's advisable to check for any specific regulations or guidelines related to the forest. Some areas may have restrictions, especially during bird nesting seasons.

Plaka Forest is a serene and captivating destination on the island of Kos, offering a respite from the typical tourist activities.

CHAPTER SEVEN

SHOPPING IN KOS

Shopping in Kos is a delightful experience that allows you to take a piece of this beautiful island home with you. Whether you're looking for traditional Greek souvenirs, unique handicrafts, fashion, or local food products, Kos offers a wide range of shopping opportunities. In this chapter, we'll guide you through the island's shopping scene and offer valuable tips to make your shopping adventure in Kos memorable.

Local Markets

Eleftherias Square Market

Location: Eleftherias Square, Kos Town

Eleftherias Square Market, nestled in the heart of Kos Town, is a lively and bustling marketplace that perfectly encapsulates the island's culinary heritage.

Fresh Produce: One of the market's primary draws is its abundant selection of fresh produce. Local farmers proudly display their harvest, which includes ripe, juicy tomatoes, succulent olives, crisp cucumbers, and much more. The market's location in the center of town means that you're getting the freshest picks directly from the region's fertile lands.

Cheeses and Dairy: Greece is renowned for its dairy products, and the market showcases an array of cheeses, such as the crumbly and tangy feta, and graviera, a hard cheese with a nutty flavor. Pair these cheeses with locally-sourced honey for a mouthwatering blend of sweet and savory.

Greek Delicacies: Tantalize your taste buds with a range of Greek delicacies. Sample pasteli, a sweet treat made from sesame seeds and honey. Dive into loukoumades, which are delightful honey-soaked doughnuts, or indulge in the rich layers of baklava, a sweet pastry made of layers of phyllo dough, honey, and crushed nuts.

Local Products: Besides fresh produce and mouthwatering delicacies, you'll also find a variety of local products. Look for extra virgin olive oils with distinct flavors, Greek wines, aromatic herbs and spices that reflect the Mediterranean landscape, and handmade soaps crafted from natural ingredients.

Old Town Market

Location: Kos Old Town

Kos Old Town is a picturesque and historic part of the island, and within it lies the captivating Old Town Market.

Handmade Jewelry: One of the highlights of the Old Town Market is the exquisite handmade jewelry. Talented local artisans create unique pieces, each telling a story through its design. From intricate filigree work to jewelry inspired by Greek mythology, there's something to cater to a wide range of tastes.

Ceramics: Kos is renowned for its pottery, and this market is an excellent place to discover beautifully hand-painted ceramics. You can find vases, plates, and amphorae adorned with intricate patterns and vivid colors. These pieces are both artistic and functional, making them meaningful souvenirs.

Textiles: The market also boasts a rich collection of handwoven textiles. From intricately patterned carpets to cozy blankets and vibrant tablecloths, these textiles showcase the island's cultural heritage. Many of these textiles are handcrafted using traditional techniques that have been passed down through generations.

Local Artworks: The Old Town Market isn't just about crafts; it's also a hub for local artworks. You'll come across paintings and artworks that depict the island's breathtaking landscapes, historic landmarks, and cultural traditions. These pieces not only beautify your space but also serve as reminders of your time in Kos.

Hippocrates Square Market

Location: Hippocrates Square, Kos Town

Hippocrates Square Market, named after the famous ancient physician Hippocrates, is another gem in Kos's shopping scene.

Traditional Greek Clothing: For those seeking traditional Greek clothing, this market is a treasure trove. You'll find shops offering embroidered blouses, tunics, and headscarves. These garments aren't just fashionable; they are also steeped in history and make for unique additions to your wardrobe.

Pottery and Ceramics: In addition to the Old Town Market, Hippocrates Square Market also features a variety of pottery and ceramics. These items range from decorative pieces like vases to functional ones like plates. Many of the designs draw inspiration from Greek culture and mythology.

Local Artifacts: If you're interested in historical artifacts, this market has a selection of items that evoke Greece's rich past. You might discover ancient-style coins, replicas of famous sculptures, and other curiosities that reflect the island's historical significance.

Local Food Products: Don't forget to explore the section dedicated to local food products. Here you can find high-quality Kos honey, fragrant olive oil, and an array of spices. These products capture the essence of the island's culinary tradition and provide a delicious way to remember your visit.

These local markets offer more than just shopping; they provide a captivating insight into the rich culture and history of Kos. Whether you're hunting for a unique gift, an addition to your home décor, or a taste of authentic Greek flavors, you'll find it within the bustling stalls of these markets.

Souvenirs and Handicrafts

When visiting Kos, it's only natural to want to bring a piece of this beautiful Greek island back home with you. Souvenirs and handicrafts from Kos are not only keepsakes but also tangible connections to the island's rich cultural heritage. In this section, we'll delve into the world of Kos's souvenirs and handicrafts, helping you understand what to look for and where to find these cherished items.

Traditional Greek Pottery

Greek pottery is renowned for its timeless beauty and intricate designs. For centuries, ceramics have played a significant role in Greek culture, both as functional items and pieces of art. When shopping for traditional Greek pottery in Kos, consider the following:

- **Types of Pottery:** You'll find a variety of pottery items, including vases, plates, bowls, and amphorae. Each piece is often adorned with motifs inspired by ancient Greek art and mythology.

- **Ceramic Techniques:** Kos is home to many talented ceramic artisans who use techniques passed down through generations. Look for hand-painted, hand-thrown, and hand-sculpted pieces that showcase the skill and creativity of these artists.

- **Color and Design:** Greek pottery often features vibrant colors, such as deep blues, rich reds, and earthy tones. Common designs include depictions of gods, goddesses, mythical creatures, and scenes from Greek mythology.

- **Functional or Decorative:** Consider whether you want a piece for everyday use, like a coffee mug, or a decorative item that will grace your home as an art piece.

- **Shopping Locations:** Pottery shops can be found throughout Kos, particularly in the Old Town of Kos. Visit local boutiques and studios to find unique and authentic pieces.

Olive Wood Products

Greece is renowned for its olive oil and, consequently, its olive trees. Olive wood is a sustainable and beautiful material used to craft a variety of items. Here's what to know about olive wood products in Kos:

- **Common Items:** Look for cutting boards, salad bowls, utensils, coasters, and even jewelry made from olive wood. These items often have a distinct and elegant grain pattern.

- **Durable and Hygienic:** Olive wood is known for its durability and natural antibacterial properties, making it an excellent choice for kitchenware.

- **Handcrafted Beauty:** Olive wood items are typically handcrafted, making each piece unique. The artisanal nature of these products adds to their charm.

- **Shopping Locations:** Many gift shops and boutiques in Kos offer a selection of olive wood items. The Old Town of Kos and the bustling markets are excellent places to start your search.

Handwoven Textiles

Kos has a rich tradition of producing handwoven textiles, including carpets, blankets, tablecloths, and other fabric items. These textiles are not only functional but also deeply rooted in Greek culture:

- **Patterns and Designs:** Greek textiles are often characterized by intricate patterns and vibrant colors. Many patterns draw inspiration from nature and local traditions.

- **Quality Materials:** Traditional textiles are made from high-quality materials like cotton, wool, and silk, ensuring their longevity and comfort.

- **Local Craftsmanship:** These textiles are often created by skilled local artisans, some of whom use age-old weaving techniques to produce these exquisite items.

- **Usage:** While some textiles are purely decorative, others are designed for everyday use. Be sure to choose textiles that suit your intended purpose.

- **Shopping Locations:** Textile shops and boutiques in the Old Town of Kos and around the island offer a wide selection of handwoven items. You can often find these textiles at local markets as well.

Leather Goods

Greece, and Kos in particular, is known for producing high-quality leather goods. If you're in the market for leather products, consider the following:

- **Items Available:** You'll find leather bags, sandals, belts, wallets, and even clothing made from premium Greek leather.

- **Quality:** Greek leather is known for its high quality and durability, making it a great investment for long-lasting accessories.

- **Style Variety:** Leather goods in Kos come in various styles, from classic and timeless to contemporary and fashionable.

- **Shopping Locations:** Many boutiques and shops in Kos Town and the Old Town specialize in leather products. Be sure to check for authenticity and quality when making a purchase.

Final Tips

When shopping for souvenirs and handicrafts in Kos, consider the following tips:

- **Authenticity:** Look for items that are genuinely made in Greece, as this ensures you're taking home an authentic piece of Greek culture.

- **Haggling:** In local markets and smaller boutiques, bargaining is common. Approach it with respect and a smile, and you may secure a better deal.

- **Local Artisans:** If possible, buy directly from local artisans or shops that support them. This helps sustain traditional crafts and benefits the local economy.

- **Packaging:** Ensure that delicate items are packaged securely to prevent damage during your journey home.

Souvenirs and handicrafts from Kos are not merely objects; they are tangible memories of your visit to this stunning Greek island. Each piece carries a part of Kos's history, culture, and natural beauty, making them cherished keepsakes for years to come.

Fashion and Boutiques

Kos, known for its pristine beaches and ancient history, is also a thriving hub for fashion and boutique shopping. From trendy beachwear to unique, handcrafted clothing and accessories.

Kos Town Shopping District

- **Agora Street:** Agora Street in Kos Town is the epicenter of fashion and boutique shopping on the island. Lined with an array of shops, from quaint boutiques to high-end fashion retailers, this bustling street offers an extensive selection of clothing, accessories, and footwear.

- **Local Designers:** Many boutiques on Agora Street showcase the work of local Greek designers. Here, you can find exclusive pieces that combine contemporary trends with traditional elements, offering a unique blend of style and culture.

- **Beachwear:** With its stunning coastline, it's no surprise that Kos excels in beachwear fashion. Beach boutiques offer a variety of swimsuits, cover-ups, and accessories that cater to every style, from boho-chic to classic elegance.

Jewelry Shops

Greek jewelry is famous for its intricate designs and meaningful symbols. When it comes to accessorizing your outfit, Kos offers a wide range of options:

- **Gold and Silver:** Jewelry shops in Kos carry exquisite gold and silver pieces, often inspired by Greek mythology, the sea, and local culture. You can find rings, necklaces, bracelets, and more, making for meaningful souvenirs or elegant gifts.

- **Gemstone Jewelry:** Kos is known for its semi-precious gemstones, and local jewelers incorporate them into their creations. From amethyst to aquamarine, you'll find stunning gemstone jewelry that captures the colors of the Mediterranean.

Tailored Clothing

Tailoring is an ancient tradition in Greece, and Kos is no exception. If you're looking for a truly unique and personalized piece of clothing, consider getting an item tailored:

- **Suits and Dresses:** Some tailors on the island specialize in crafting custom suits, dresses, and formalwear. You can choose the fabric, design, and details to create a one-of-a-kind garment.

- **Alterations:** Many tailors in Kos also offer alteration services. If you've found the perfect piece but it doesn't fit quite right, they can adjust it to your specifications.

Shopping Tips

When shopping for fashion in Kos, keep the following tips in mind:

- **Local Materials:** Seek out items made from local materials like linen and cotton. These fabrics are ideal for the warm Mediterranean climate and carry the essence of Greek fashion.

- **Haggling:** While haggling is common in some markets, it's not typical in fashion boutiques. Prices are generally fixed in these establishments.

- **Sizing:** Pay attention to sizing, as Greek sizing can differ from what you're used to. Be sure to try items on when possible or ask the sales staff for guidance.

- **Local Brands:** Explore local Greek brands that may not be available in your home country. These brands often offer unique styles you won't find elsewhere.

Overall, Kos's fashion and boutique scene is as diverse and stylish as the island itself.

Bargaining Tips in Kos

When visiting markets, street vendors, or even some small shops in various destinations, knowing how to bargain can be incredibly useful

Start with a Friendly Greeting

- When entering a shop or market stall, greet the seller with a warm and friendly "Kalimera" (good morning) or "Kalispera" (good evening), depending on the time of day. Building a positive rapport from the beginning sets the tone for a more pleasant bargaining experience.

Do Your Research

- Before you start haggling, it's essential to have a general idea of the item's value. Research the typical price range for the product you're interested in to ensure you have a reasonable starting point for negotiation.

Keep a Friendly Demeanor

- Politeness goes a long way in bargaining. Smile, maintain eye contact, and be respectful when making your offer. It's about building a connection and finding a mutual agreement.

Don't Show Overeagerness

- Avoid displaying too much enthusiasm for the item you want to purchase. Sellers may increase their prices if they sense you really want it. Maintain a sense of detachment and casual interest.

Start with a Low Counteroffer

- When the seller states the initial price, politely counter with an offer significantly lower than your target price. This allows room for negotiation while showing your intention to get a good deal.

Be Willing to Walk Away

- If the seller's counteroffer doesn't align with your budget or expectations, be prepared to walk away. Often, the vendor will call you back with a better offer to close the sale.

Use Cash

- Cash payments often give you an advantage in bargaining. Credit cards and other electronic payment methods may not be as flexible when it comes to discounts.

Bundle Items for Better Deals

- If you plan to buy multiple items from the same vendor, consider negotiating for a package deal. Vendors may be more willing to lower the overall price when selling in bulk.

Know When to Stop

- While bargaining can be fun and rewarding, it's important to recognize when you've reached a reasonable agreement. Pushing too hard or bargaining too long may sour the interaction or lead to a missed opportunity.

Respect Local Customs

- Be aware that bargaining isn't suitable for all situations, especially in more upscale shops and restaurants. It's best reserved for markets, stalls, and smaller stores.

In conclusion, shopping in Kos is not just about buying things; it's an opportunity to immerse yourself in the island's culture and take home a piece of its unique charm. Enjoy your shopping experience in this beautiful Greek paradise.

CHAPTER EIGHT

FESTIVALS AND EVENTS

Kos, with its rich cultural heritage and vibrant local life, hosts a variety of festivals and events throughout the year. These celebrations provide visitors with a unique opportunity to immerse themselves in the island's traditions, experience its lively atmosphere, and create lasting memories. In this chapter, we'll delve into the most significant festivals and events that you can enjoy during your visit to Kos.

Annual Festivals

In this section, we explore some of the island's most significant annual festivals that offer a glimpse into the heart and soul of Kos.

Carnival (Apokries)
When: February/March

Carnival in Kos - A Riot of Color and Celebration

Carnival, known as "Apokries" in Greek, is a time of revelry and celebration on the island of Kos. The festivities typically begin several weeks before Lent, building up to a crescendo during the Carnival weekend. Kos Town becomes the epicenter of the celebrations, where locals and visitors come together for a joyous and colorful experience.

Elaborate Costumes: The heart of the Carnival season is the Carnival parade. This parade is a dazzling display of creativity and imagination, with participants donning elaborate and often humorous costumes. From mythological characters to pop culture icons, you'll be amazed at the diversity and ingenuity on display.

Street Parties and Music: The streets of Kos Town come alive with vibrant street parties, live music, and dancing. It's a time when the entire community unites to celebrate life and let loose. The lively atmosphere is infectious, and you'll find yourself tapping your feet to the Greek music and joining in the spontaneous dances that break out.

Traditional Foods and Sweets: No Greek celebration is complete without indulging in delicious food. During Carnival, you'll find an array of traditional Greek dishes and sweets to savor. From souvlaki to loukoumades (sweet doughnuts), your taste buds are in for a treat.

Ouzo and Wine: As with most Greek celebrations, Carnival is an occasion to enjoy good company and raise a glass. Ouzo, the famous anise-flavored spirit, flows freely, and local wines are also savored. It's a time for socializing, laughter, and creating lasting memories.

Carnival in Kos is a time when the island lets its hair down, and the sense of community and togetherness is palpable. Whether you're in it for the artistic costumes, the lively music, or the delectable food, Carnival in Kos promises an unforgettable experience.

Easter (Pascha)
When: April

Easter in Kos - A Spiritual and Cultural Celebration

Easter is a deeply religious and highly anticipated celebration throughout Greece, and Kos, with its strong Orthodox Christian traditions, is no exception. The Easter season is a time of profound significance, marked by a blend of spirituality, family gatherings, and cultural rituals.

Midnight Services: The heart of the Easter celebration in Kos is the midnight Resurrection service, which takes place in the island's churches. Attending this service is a deeply spiritual and cultural experience. Worshippers hold candles and gather around the church to mark the Resurrection of Christ.

Fireworks and Red Eggs: The announcement of Christ's Resurrection is a breathtaking moment. The sky is illuminated by a spectacular display of colorful fireworks, and people exchange red-dyed eggs. The tradition is to engage in "tsougrisma," a game where two people attempt to crack each other's eggs. The person whose egg remains unbroken is said to have good luck.

Easter Feast: Easter Sunday is a time for families to come together and share a hearty feast. The centerpiece of this meal is often lamb, roasted to perfection. Accompanying the lamb is "tsoureki," a sweet Easter bread, and a variety of other traditional dishes. The Easter table is a true feast for the senses.

Local Customs: Easter in Kos is a time when you can witness and participate in local customs. From the midnight Resurrection service to the cracking of red eggs, you'll get a taste of the island's deep-rooted traditions.

Easter is a time when the island is steeped in tradition, and visitors have the unique opportunity to witness the profound religious devotion of the locals. It's a time of reflection, celebration, and an appreciation of the island's rich cultural heritage.

Hippokratia Festival
When: July

The Hippokratia Festival, one of the most unique and culturally significant events on the island of Kos, is an annual celebration that pays homage to Hippocrates, the Father of Medicine. Hippocrates was born on this very island around 460 BC, and his contributions to the field of medicine are celebrated throughout the festival. Visitors to Kos during this time are treated to a captivating blend of culture, history, and modern medical exploration.

What to Expect:

1. Medical Conferences:

The heart of the Hippokratia Festival lies in its medical conferences. The island of Kos, with its historical significance in the world of medicine, hosts renowned healthcare professionals, medical researchers, and students from around the globe. These conferences serve as a platform for the exchange of knowledge, ideas, and innovations in the field of medicine. It's a unique opportunity to witness the evolution of medicine in the place where it all began.

2. Art and Culture:

Beyond the realm of medicine, the festival also showcases the island's cultural heritage. Art exhibitions featuring local artists and their works can be found throughout the island during the festival. The themes often revolve around health, healing, and the legacy of Hippocrates. It's a chance to appreciate the artistic talent of the island while reflecting on the historical importance of medical knowledge.

3. Music and Entertainment:

The Hippokratia Festival is not all about science and art; it's also a time for joy and celebration. You can expect live music performances, cultural events, and entertaining activities for both locals and visitors. The festival provides a lively and festive atmosphere, bringing people together to celebrate the island's heritage.

4. Exploring Hippocrates' Legacy:

Visiting the Asclepius Sanctuary, where Hippocrates received his early education, is an essential part of the festival. You can explore the ancient ruins, which are said to have played a pivotal role in the development of medical knowledge. The festival often features guided tours of these historical sites, offering valuable insights into the birthplace of modern medicine.

The Hippokratia Festival is an extraordinary opportunity for travelers to delve into the history of medicine, gain a deeper appreciation for the island's rich cultural heritage, and experience the intellectual side of Kos. It is a celebration that bridges the past and present, highlighting the enduring legacy of Hippocrates while fostering innovation and collaboration in the medical field. If you have a passion for medicine, history, or simply wish to partake in a truly unique cultural experience, the Hippokratia Festival in Kos is not to be missed.

Cultural Celebrations in Kos

In this section, we will explore some of the most captivating cultural celebrations that take place on the island of Kos.

Antimacheia Folk Festival

When: August

The Antimacheia Folk Festival, held annually in August, is a vibrant celebration of Greek culture that beautifully encapsulates the island's heritage. This event is a fantastic opportunity for visitors to connect with the locals, experience traditional Greek music and dance, and immerse themselves in the island's rich cultural traditions.

Highlights

Traditional Greek Music

The heart of the Antimacheia Folk Festival lies in the enchanting sounds of traditional Greek music. Local musicians, often with traditional instruments such as the bouzouki and lyre, take center stage to serenade the crowd with their captivating melodies. The hauntingly beautiful tunes resonate with a sense of history and the deep cultural roots of Greece.

Dance Performances

No Greek festival is complete without lively dance performances. At the Antimacheia Folk Festival, you'll have the opportunity to witness traditional Greek dances featuring energetic movements and colorful costumes. The dancers' enthusiasm is infectious, and you might even find yourself encouraged to join in the dance, experiencing the joy of this centuries-old tradition.

Local Cuisine

Greek festivals are synonymous with delicious food, and the Antimacheia Folk Festival is no exception. Food stalls and vendors offer an array of authentic Greek dishes and local specialties. From moussaka to souvlaki, and baklava to loukoumades (honey-soaked donuts), you can savor a true culinary delight that will tantalize your taste buds.

Participate in the Festivities

One of the most endearing aspects of this festival is the warm and inviting nature of the locals. They're not just content with having you as spectators; they often encourage visitors to participate in the festivities. Whether it's trying your hand at traditional Greek dance steps or learning about the history and significance of the music, the festival is a welcoming experience that will make you feel like part of the local community.

The Antimacheia Folk Festival is a kaleidoscope of Greek culture, offering a unique opportunity to dive headfirst into the island's traditions and experience the vibrant spirit of the locals.

Wine Festivals

When: Various

Kos's wine festivals are a testament to the island's deep-rooted love for viticulture and winemaking. Throughout the year, several villages on the island host wine festivals, and these events are a paradise for wine enthusiasts and those interested in exploring the world of Greek wines.

Highlights

Wine Tasting: The heart of any wine festival is, of course, the opportunity to savor a wide variety of local wines. From crisp, refreshing whites to robust, full-bodied reds, you can sample wines produced by the island's vineyards. Many of these vineyards have been producing wines for generations, and experts are often on hand to provide insights into the winemaking process.

Greek Gastronomy: Wine and food are the perfect companions, and these festivals offer a delightful chance to pair your wine with authentic Greek cuisine. You can explore local dishes and delicacies that complement the wines beautifully. Whether it's pairing a bold red with succulent lamb dishes or a crisp white with fresh seafood, the combination of wine and Greek gastronomy is a culinary journey in itself.

Live Entertainment: The festival experience extends beyond wine and food, with lively entertainment in the form of music and dance performances. Greek music, often accompanied by traditional instruments like the bouzouki, fills the air, creating a festive and celebratory atmosphere. The locals love to dance, and you'll often find yourself tapping your feet and swaying to the rhythm.

Learn About Winemaking: Many of these wine festivals offer educational opportunities for visitors. Wine experts and winemakers are usually present to explain the art of winemaking, from grape cultivation to the bottling process. This educational aspect can deepen your appreciation for the island's wine culture and help you understand the unique characteristics of Kos wines.

Kos's wine festivals are not just about wine; they're a holistic experience that combines wine appreciation, Greek gastronomy, live entertainment, and an opportunity to learn about the island's winemaking traditions.

Sardine Festival (Sardelopoula)
When: September

The Sardine Festival, locally known as "Sardelopoula," is a delightful and distinctive cultural celebration that captures the heart of the maritime culture in Kos. Set against the backdrop of the beautiful Aegean Sea, this festival is a tribute to the island's strong connection to the bounties of the sea and the age-old tradition of fishing. It's an event that promises visitors an unforgettable experience, filled with the tantalizing aromas and vibrant colors of Mediterranean cuisine and the exuberant spirit of Greek hospitality.

Highlights

Fresh Sardines in Abundance: The star of the Sardine Festival is, of course, the sardine itself. These small, flavorful fish are freshly caught from the nearby waters and prepared in a variety of mouthwatering ways. Grilled sardines, marinated sardines, sardine saganaki (a savory dish cooked with tomatoes and cheese), and many more sardine-based delights are on offer. It's a seafood lover's dream come true. The unique taste of sardines, seasoned with local herbs and olive oil, provides a true taste of the Mediterranean.

Lively Music and Dance: Greek festivals are known for their lively and spirited atmosphere, and the Sardine Festival is no exception. Traditional Greek music, often accompanied by instruments like the bouzouki, fills the air. Local musicians and dancers take the stage, performing traditional Greek dances. The energetic movements, colorful costumes, and inviting melodies create a contagious sense of celebration. Visitors are often encouraged to join in the dance, making it a great way to experience the warmth and inclusiveness of Greek culture.

Cultural Experience: Beyond the delicious food and lively entertainment, the Sardine Festival provides an opportunity to delve into the maritime traditions of Kos. You can witness local fishermen at work, repairing nets and preparing their boats for the next catch. It's a fascinating look into the island's fishing history and its vital role in the community's identity. The festival offers a chance to learn about the methods and tools used in traditional fishing, and the importance of the sea in the daily life of Kos.

Souvenirs and Crafts: Local artisans often set up stalls to showcase their handicrafts and souvenirs. This is an excellent place to pick up unique gifts and keepsakes, from handmade jewelry to intricate ceramics. It's an opportunity to take home a piece of Kos's culture and artistic heritage.

Overall, the Sardine Festival is a wonderful example of how Kos celebrates its connection to the sea and the importance of maritime traditions.

Religious Events

Kos, like the rest of Greece, has a rich tradition of religious events and festivals that play a vital role in the island's cultural and spiritual life. These events are not only significant for the local population but also offer a unique and immersive experience for visitors interested in understanding the island's deep-rooted religious traditions. In this section, we will explore some of the most important religious events that take place in Kos.

Assumption of Mary (Panagia)
When: August 15

The Assumption of Mary, known as Panagia in Greek, is one of the most important religious events in Kos. It commemorates the belief that the Virgin Mary, the mother of Jesus, was taken bodily into heaven. This event is celebrated with great devotion, and it has both religious and cultural significance. Here's what you can expect:

Church Services: On the day of Panagia, churches across the island hold special services, with the most notable one taking place in the Church of Panagia tis Mesi, which is beautifully decorated for the occasion.

Religious Processions: Religious processions are an integral part of the celebrations. Images of the Virgin Mary are paraded through the streets, accompanied by clergy and the local community. The faithful follow in procession, often holding candles or flowers.

Traditional Feasts: After the religious ceremonies, it's customary to enjoy a festive meal with family and friends. Traditional Greek dishes and sweets are prepared, and it's a time for people to come together and share in the joy of the occasion.

Saint John's Day (Aghios Ioannis)
When: June 24

Aghios Ioannis, or Saint John, is another significant religious event in Kos. It's celebrated on June 24th and is associated with the feast day of John the Baptist. This event carries a special significance for the island's faithful and offers a chance for visitors to witness a unique local tradition:

Religious Observance: The day begins with a special religious service held at the Church of Aghios Ioannis, located in the village of Kefalos. The church is beautifully adorned with flowers and candles for the occasion.

Pilgrimage: Many pilgrims from Kos and other parts of Greece make their way to the Church of Aghios Ioannis to participate in the religious service. This creates a sense of unity and devotion.

Music and Festivities: Following the religious ceremonies, the atmosphere becomes festive. Live music, traditional dance, and local cuisine make the celebration lively and enjoyable. It's a time for the local community to come together and welcome visitors.

In conclusion, Kos's festivals and events offer a window into the island's soul, allowing you to immerse yourself in its culture, history, and spirituality. Whether you're a fan of lively parades, traditional dance, or religious rituals, the island's diverse calendar of events has something for everyone. Be sure to check the dates of these festivals and events when planning your visit to Kos to enhance your cultural experience.

CHAPTER NINE

DAY TRIPS AND EXCURSIONS

Kos is not only a destination filled with its own unique treasures but also serves as an excellent base for exploring nearby islands and attractions in the region. This chapter will help you plan day trips and excursions, opening doors to new adventures beyond the island's shores.

Nearby Islands

Kos is surrounded by a cluster of stunning islands, each with its own unique charm. These nearby islands make for perfect day trips from Kos, and in this section, we'll introduce you to three of them.

Nisyros Island

Location: Approximately 37 kilometers southwest of Kos.

Why Visit Nisyros?

Nisyros is a volcanic island that promises a truly unique and unforgettable experience. With its active volcano and charming villages, this nearby island is a must-visit for those seeking natural wonders and authentic Greek culture.

What to Do on Nisyros

- **Explore the Volcano**: Witness the otherworldly landscape of the Stefanos Crater. You can hike to the crater's edge and peer into the sulfurous fumaroles, a true geological wonder.

- **Mandraki Village**: Meander through the narrow streets of Mandraki, the island's main village. Admire the whitewashed houses with colorful doors and windows, and enjoy a cup of Greek coffee in one of the local cafes.

- **Local Cuisine**: Savor the island's local cuisine, which often features Nisyros' own fresh produce and unique flavors. Don't miss a taste of "pitaridia," a traditional dish made with chickpeas.

Travel Tips

- **Ferry Services**: Nisyros is easily accessible from Kos by ferry. Be sure to check the ferry schedules in advance.

- **Hiking**: If you plan to hike the volcano, wear appropriate footwear, and bring plenty of water and sun protection.

- **Photography**: The volcanic landscapes of Nisyros are a photographer's paradise, so don't forget your camera.

-

Kalymnos Island

Location: Situated 35 kilometers north of Kos.

Why Visit Kalymnos?

Kalymnos, known as the "Sponge Divers' Island," is an adventurer's paradise. The island is famous for its sponge diving heritage and offers a range of outdoor activities and natural beauty.

What to Do on Kalymnos

- **Rock Climbing**: Kalymnos is a renowned rock climbing destination. Whether you're a beginner or an experienced climber, you'll find routes for all levels.

- **Maritime Adventures**: Enjoy crystal-clear waters by snorkeling, scuba diving, or sailing. You can also take a boat trip to explore secluded coves and beaches.

- **Sponge Trade**: Explore the local sponge industry and learn about the island's history as a sponge-diving hub.

Travel Tips

- **Rock Climbing**: If you're interested in rock climbing, consider booking a guided tour or renting equipment from one of the local climbing schools.

- **Seafood Feast**: Don't miss the opportunity to savor fresh seafood at one of Kalymnos' seaside tavernas.

Symi Island

Location: Symi is located approximately 37 kilometers northwest of Kos.

Why Visit Symi?

Symi is renowned for its neoclassical architecture, colorful houses, and tranquil ambiance. This island provides a charming contrast to the bustling streets of Kos Town.

What to Do on Symi

- **Symi Harbor**: Wander along the picturesque harbor of Symi, surrounded by neoclassical buildings painted in pastel shades. Visit the local shops and cafes.

- **Panormitis Monastery**: A trip to Symi isn't complete without visiting the Panormitis Monastery, a significant religious site with stunning architecture and a peaceful atmosphere.

- **Beach Relaxation**: Enjoy the island's beautiful beaches, like Nanou Beach and Marathounda Beach, where you can swim and unwind.

Travel Tips

- **Ferry Schedule**: Check the ferry schedule for daily trips to Symi from Kos and back. It's advisable to book your tickets in advance during the peak tourist season.

- **Monastery Etiquette**: When visiting the Panormitis Monastery, dress modestly and be respectful of the religious significance of the site.

Visiting these nearby islands from Kos provides a wonderful opportunity to diversify your Greek island adventure, offering you unique experiences, natural beauty, and cultural insights.

Exploring the Dodecanese

The Dodecanese is an enchanting archipelago in the southeastern Aegean Sea, comprised of numerous islands, each with its unique charm and character. Kos, one of the most prominent islands in the group, serves as an ideal springboard for exploring the treasures of the Dodecanese. In this section, we will delve into some of the most captivating islands in the Dodecanese, each offering a distinctive experience waiting to be discovered.

Rhodes

Why Visit Rhodes? Rhodes is a magnificent island, known for its historical significance, beautiful beaches, and vibrant atmosphere. Whether you're interested in exploring ancient history or simply relaxing on the shore, Rhodes has something for everyone.

What to See and Do:

- **Rhodes Old Town:** The heart of Rhodes is its captivating Old Town, a UNESCO World Heritage site. Inside its medieval walls, you'll find a labyrinth of cobblestone streets, historic buildings, and charming squares. Don't miss the Palace of the Grand Master, a stunning medieval castle.

- **Lindos:** Located on the eastern coast of Rhodes, Lindos is a charming village with narrow streets and white-washed houses. The Acropolis of Lindos stands atop a hill and offers a splendid view of the surrounding area.

- **Beaches:** Rhodes boasts a variety of beautiful beaches. Tsambika Beach is known for its golden sand, while Faliraki is a bustling beach with water sports and beach bars. Anthony Quinn Bay is a tranquil cove with clear waters perfect for snorkeling.

- **Nightlife:** Rhodes Town comes alive at night. You can enjoy a lively nightlife scene with numerous bars, clubs, and restaurants, where you can dance the night away.

Patmos
Why Visit Patmos? Patmos is a tranquil and spiritually significant island, revered for its spiritual heritage and

serene beauty. It's an ideal destination for those looking to explore religious history and enjoy peaceful surroundings.

What to See and Do:

- **Cave of the Apocalypse:** This sacred cave is a must-visit for religious pilgrims. It is believed to be the place where Saint John received the divine Revelation, making it an essential destination for spiritual seekers.

- **Monastery of Saint John the Theologian:** A UNESCO World Heritage site, this stunning monastery features Byzantine architecture and is home to priceless religious artifacts.

- **Chora:** The island's main town, Chora, is a delightful place to explore with its white-washed buildings, narrow streets, and charming local restaurants.

- **Beaches:** Patmos offers a selection of serene beaches such as Psili Ammos and Lambi Beach, perfect for relaxation and swimming.

Leros

Why Visit Leros? Leros is a hidden gem, where history intertwines with breathtaking landscapes. This island is a quiet escape, known for its rich history and natural beauty.

What to See and Do:

- **Agia Marina:** This picturesque fishing village is the main port of Leros. Stroll through its charming streets, visit the medieval castle, and enjoy the local atmosphere.

- **Lakki:** Lakki, a unique feature on Leros, is characterized by its Art Deco architecture. It's a perfect place to explore and learn about the island's past.

- **War Tunnels:** Leros bears the scars of World War II, and you can explore the tunnels carved by the Italians during the conflict. These tunnels offer insight into the island's wartime history.

- **Beaches:** Leros features some lovely beaches, including Vromolithos and Alinda, where you can enjoy the tranquility of the Aegean Sea and perhaps try some water sports.

Each of these islands in the Dodecanese offers a distinct experience, from the historical grandeur of Rhodes to the spiritual significance of Patmos and the peaceful ambiance and natural beauty of Leros. Exploring these neighboring islands from Kos allows you to immerse yourself in the unique character of each destination.

Historical Sites Beyond Kos

While Kos itself is brimming with historical and archaeological treasures, the nearby regions offer a wealth of fascinating historical sites that are easily accessible for day trips. These excursions will take you on a journey through time, unveiling the rich history of the Dodecanese and neighboring areas. In this section, we'll delve into some of the most significant historical sites beyond Kos.

Ephesus, Turkey

Ephesus, located just a boat ride away from Kos, is one of the most well-preserved ancient cities in the Mediterranean. It boasts a rich history, dating back to the 10th century BC, when it was an important Ionian city. Here's what you can explore:

The Library of Celsus: The Library of Celsus is an iconic structure in Ephesus. This ancient library once held thousands of scrolls and was an architectural marvel of its time. Its façade, adorned with statues and intricate carvings, is a testament to the grandeur of the city.

The Great Theater: The Great Theater in Ephesus is an enormous amphitheater that could accommodate up to 25,000 spectators. It was a venue for various performances, including gladiatorial contests and dramas.

Visitors can still admire its remarkable acoustics and architecture.

Temple of Artemis: One of the Seven Wonders of the Ancient World, the Temple of Artemis was a magnificent structure dedicated to the Greek goddess Artemis. While only a few columns remain, it offers a glimpse into the past grandeur of the city.

Bodrum, Turkey

Bodrum, a charming Turkish coastal town, is a short ferry ride from Kos. It's not only a picturesque destination but also home to several historical sites:

The Mausoleum at Halicarnassus: The Mausoleum at Halicarnassus was the final resting place of Mausolus, a ruler of Caria, and his sister Artemisia. This grand tomb, featuring intricate sculptures and architectural brilliance, is considered one of the Seven Wonders of the Ancient World.

Bodrum Castle (Castle of St. Peter): Bodrum Castle is a well-preserved medieval fortress constructed by the Knights Hospitaller in the 15th century. It now houses the Museum of Underwater Archaeology, showcasing artifacts from shipwrecks and maritime history.

Bodrum Amphitheater: The ancient Bodrum Amphitheater offers stunning views of the town and the sea. It's a well-preserved relic of ancient Halicarnassus, accommodating around 13,000 spectators during its prime.

Knidos, Turkey

Knidos, located on the Datça Peninsula in Turkey, is just a short boat ride from Kos and offers a unique historical experience:

Temple of Aphrodite: The Temple of Aphrodite is an ancient sanctuary dedicated to the Greek goddess of love and beauty. Its stunning location at the tip of the Datça Peninsula provides breathtaking views of the Mediterranean.

Amphitheater: Knidos boasts a well-preserved amphitheater with a seating capacity of approximately 5,000 people. This theater, which dates back to the 4th century BC, once hosted various performances and is a testament to Knidos's rich history.

Ancient Harbor and Lighthouse: The ancient harbor of Knidos, along with the remnants of its lighthouse, offers a glimpse into the city's maritime history and importance as a trade center in antiquity.

Exploring these historical sites beyond Kos is a rewarding adventure for history enthusiasts and travelers seeking a deeper understanding of the ancient world. While you marvel at the impressive architecture and historical significance of these sites, you'll also enjoy the picturesque landscapes and coastal beauty that the region has to offer.

Planning Your Day Trips

When it comes to planning day trips and excursions from Kos, meticulous preparation can make the difference between a fantastic adventure and a stressful experience. In this section, we'll cover the essential aspects of planning your day trips, ensuring you make the most of your time and enjoy a hassle-free exploration.

Booking Tours

If you prefer a guided experience with expert insights and convenience, consider booking day trips through local tour agencies or online platforms. Here are some tips:

- **Research Tour Operators:** Look for reputable tour operators with good reviews and a track record of quality service.

- **Check Inclusions:** Ensure you understand what's included in the tour package – transportation, meals, entrance fees, and any additional activities.

- **Read Reviews:** Read reviews and ratings from previous travelers to get a sense of the tour's quality.

- **Compare Prices:** Compare prices from different tour operators to find the best value for your money.

Here are some popular booking tour websites and platforms where you can find a wide range of tours and activities for your travel adventures

- **TripAdvisor   Experiences (www.tripadvisor.com/Attractions):** TripAdvisor offers user-generated reviews and ratings for tours and attractions. You can book directly through their platform based on recommendations from fellow travelers.
- **Viator (www.viator.com):** Viator is a global leader in providing tours, activities, and experiences in various destinations around the world. You can find a diverse selection of options, from guided tours to skip-the-line tickets.

Transportation

Depending on your chosen destinations, transportation can vary. Here's how to handle it:

- **Ferry Schedules:** Research and note the ferry schedules to and from your destination. Be sure to check return times to avoid getting stranded.

- **Ticket Reservations:** If possible, book ferry or boat tickets in advance, especially during peak tourist seasons, to secure your seat.

- **Travel Documents:** Ensure you have all the necessary travel documents, including passports, visas, and any required permits, especially when traveling to nearby Turkish destinations.

Pack Smart

Packing is crucial to ensure your comfort and preparedness during day trips. Here's what to consider:

- **Weather-Appropriate Attire:** Dress according to the weather forecast. Pack layers for changing temperatures and rain gear if necessary.

- **Comfortable Footwear:** Wear comfortable walking shoes, as you might be exploring historical sites, trails, or beaches.

- **Swimsuit and Towel:** If you plan to swim, snorkel, or enjoy water activities, pack your swimsuit, a towel, and any necessary beach gear.

- **Sun Protection:** Bring sunscreen, sunglasses, a hat, and a reusable water bottle to stay hydrated.

Respect Local Culture

When visiting nearby islands, historical sites, or other destinations, it's essential to be culturally sensitive:

- **Research Local Customs:** Familiarize yourself with the local customs and etiquette of the places you'll be visiting. Different regions may have unique practices.

- **Dress Modestly:** In some destinations, particularly religious sites, dress modestly by covering shoulders and knees.

- **Photography Etiquette:** Always ask for permission before taking photos, especially of people, and respect areas where photography is prohibited.

Time Management

Efficient time management ensures you make the most of your day trips:

- **Plan Your Itinerary:** Create a rough itinerary for your day trip, allowing time for sightseeing, relaxation, and meals.

- **Consider Travel Time:** Factor in travel time to and from your destination, as well as the time required for activities.

- **Arrive Early:** Aim to arrive at the ferry terminal or starting point early to avoid any last-minute rushes.

With thoughtful planning, you can embark on your day trips and excursions from Kos with confidence, knowing that you've taken care of all the important details.

CHAPTER TEN

PRACTICAL INFORMATON

As you prepare for your unforgettable journey to Kos, it's essential to have practical information at your fingertips. This chapter covers everything you need to know to ensure a smooth and enjoyable visit to this Greek paradise.

Visa and Entry Requirements

Before you embark on your trip to Kos, it's crucial to check the visa and entry requirements, depending on your nationality. Here's what you should keep in mind:

- **Visa Requirements**: Greece is part of the Schengen Area, which means that most EU and EEA citizens don't need a visa for short visits. However, it's vital to verify the latest requirements with the Greek embassy or consulate in your home country.

- **Passport Validity**: Ensure that your passport is valid for at least three months beyond your planned departure from Greece.

- **Visa-Free Countries**: Citizens of countries like the United States, Canada, Australia, and the UK can enter Greece for up to 90 days for tourism or business purposes without a visa.

Currency and Money Matters

Understanding the local currency and financial aspects is essential for a hassle-free trip:

- **Currency**: The official currency of Greece is the Euro (EUR). ATMs are widely available across the island, and credit cards are accepted in most hotels, restaurants, and shops.

- **Currency Exchange**: You can exchange currency at banks, exchange offices, or use ATMs to withdraw local currency.

- **Tipping**: Tipping is common in Greece. In restaurants, it's customary to leave a tip of around 10% of the bill. For other services, like taxi drivers and tour guides, a small tip is appreciated.

- **Budgeting**: While Kos offers a range of options for travelers on different budgets, it's a good idea to set a daily budget for food, activities, and souvenirs to ensure your spending stays on track.

Health and Safety Tips

Staying healthy and safe during your trip is a top priority:

- **Travel Insurance**: Consider purchasing comprehensive travel insurance to cover any unexpected medical expenses and emergencies.

- **Healthcare**: Kos has a well-developed healthcare system. There are public hospitals and private clinics. The European Health Insurance Card (EHIC) is also valid for EU citizens, offering access to state healthcare.

- **Safety**: Kos is generally a safe destination. Still, exercise standard safety precautions like safeguarding your belongings, avoiding poorly lit areas at night, and being aware of your surroundings.

- **Emergency Numbers**: The emergency number for police is 100, for fire is 199, and for medical emergencies, call 166.

- **Sun Protection**: Given the sunny Mediterranean climate, remember to pack sunscreen, sunglasses, and a wide-brimmed hat to protect yourself from the sun.

Communication

Staying connected while in Kos is essential:

- **Mobile Networks**: Greece has excellent mobile network coverage. Purchase a local SIM card or check with your provider for international roaming options.

- **Wi-Fi**: Most hotels, restaurants, and cafes in Kos offer free Wi-Fi, making it easy to stay connected.

- **Useful Phrases**: While many locals speak English, it's polite to learn a few basic Greek phrases such as "hello" (Yassas), "thank you" (Efharisto), and "please" (Parakalo).

Getting Around Kos

- **Transportation**: Renting a car, scooter, or ATV is a popular way to explore the island. Public transportation, including buses, is also reliable and economical.

- **Driving**: In Greece, you drive on the right side of the road. Remember to carry your driver's license, vehicle rental papers, and an international driving permit if required.

- **Biking and Walking**: Kos offers beautiful landscapes for biking and walking. Remember to stay hydrated, wear sunscreen, and use a map or GPS app to navigate.

Accommodation

- **Accommodation Types**: Kos offers a wide range of accommodations, from luxury resorts and boutique hotels to budget-friendly hostels and rental apartments.

- **Booking in Advance**: During the peak season, it's wise to book your accommodation in advance to secure the best options.

- **Check-in and Check-out**: Standard check-in time is around 2:00 PM, and check-out is usually by 12:00 PM.

Local Etiquette

- **Dress Code**: Dress modestly when visiting religious sites, and wear appropriate attire in restaurants and bars.

- **Greetings**: Greeks often greet with a warm handshake and a smile. "Kalimera" means "good morning," "Kalispera" means "good evening," and "Efharisto" means "thank you."

- **Respect Religious Customs**: Be respectful when visiting churches and monasteries. Women should cover their shoulders and avoid short skirts.

Language

- Official Language: The official language is Greek. While many locals in tourist areas speak English, learning a few basic Greek phrases can enhance your experience.

Time Zone

- Kos follows Eastern European Time (EET), which is UTC+2 in the winter and UTC+3 in the summer (during daylight saving time).

Electrical Outlets

- Greece uses Type C and Type F electrical outlets, with a standard voltage of 230V and a frequency of 50Hz. Be sure to bring the appropriate adapters and voltage converters if needed.

Useful Websites and Resources for Your Kos Trip

Planning your trip to Kos, Greece, can be an exciting but sometimes daunting task. To ensure your journey is as smooth and enjoyable as possible, we've compiled a list of useful websites and resources that will help you make the most of your visit to this stunning island. From transportation to accommodation, and everything in between, these resources are essential for every traveler.

Travel and Accommodation Booking

Booking.com: This well-known platform offers a vast selection of accommodation options in Kos, ranging from luxury resorts to budget-friendly hostels. You can read guest reviews and easily make reservations online.

Airbnb: If you're looking for unique and local accommodation experiences, Airbnb provides various choices, including apartments, houses, and even private rooms.

TripAdvisor: Use TripAdvisor to compare hotel prices, read traveler reviews, and get recommendations on the best places to stay in Kos.

Hostelworld: Ideal for budget travelers, Hostelworld lists and reviews hostels and affordable guesthouses on the island.

Transportation

Kos International Airport (Hippocrates): Stay updated on flight schedules, services, and transportation options to and from Kos Airport.

Ferries in Greece: Plan your ferry journeys from Kos to other Greek islands or the mainland, and book tickets in advance.

Kos Bus Services: Information about the local bus system in Kos, including schedules and routes.

Car Rentals in Kos: Renting a car can be a great way to explore the island at your own pace. Compare rental options and book in advance.

Local Transportation Apps

Moovit: If you plan to use public transportation, Moovit is a useful app for real-time transit information, routes, and schedules.

Google Maps: Download offline maps of Kos on Google Maps for navigation, location sharing, and exploring the island without a data connection.

Local News and Weather

Kos News: Stay updated with the latest news and events happening on the island.

Weather in Kos: Get accurate and up-to-date weather forecasts for Kos to help plan your daily activities.

Travel Forums and Communities

TripAdvisor Forums - Kos: Explore the TripAdvisor forums to ask questions and share your experiences with other travelers.

Language and Communication

Google Translate: If you're not familiar with Greek, Google Translate can be a lifesaver for quick translations.

Greek Phrasebook: Learn some basic Greek phrases to enhance your travel experience and connect with locals.

Money and Currency

Xe Currency Converter: Keep track of exchange rates and convert your currency to Euros, the local currency in Greece, before and during your trip.

When dealing with local currency, it's a good idea to have a small amount of cash on hand for small purchases, as some places may not accept cards. Major credit cards are widely accepted, but it's essential to inform your bank about your travel dates to avoid any issues with card usage abroad.

Dining and Food

Kos Restaurants on TripAdvisor: Explore a variety of dining options on TripAdvisor, read reviews, and find the best places to enjoy Greek cuisine.

Greek Food Guide: Familiarize yourself with Greek cuisine, its dishes, and culinary customs to make the most of your dining experiences.

Emergency Contacts

- **Emergency Services (Police, Fire, Ambulance)**: In Greece, dial 112 for any emergency services. Save this number in your phone for quick access.
- **Tourist Police**: (0030) 22420 22444 - The Tourist Police can assist travelers with various issues, including lost documents and emergencies.

Offline Maps and Travel Apps

- Before your trip, download offline maps or travel apps like Google Maps, MAPS.ME, or TripIt to navigate Kos without relying on constant internet access. These apps often provide recommendations for nearby attractions, restaurants, and accommodations as well.

Obtaining physical maps of Kos can be a valuable resource for navigating the region and exploring its attractions. Here are several places where you can typically find physical maps:

- **Tourist Information Centers:** Visit local tourist information centers in towns and villages throughout Kos. These centers often provide free or low-cost maps and brochures that include information about local attractions, accommodations, and activities.
- **Hotels and Accommodations:** Many hotels and accommodations in Kos offer complimentary maps to their guests. If you're staying at a hotel, ask at the front desk if they have maps available.

With these tools at your disposal, your trip to Kos will be more enjoyable and worry-free, allowing you to focus on creating unforgettable memories on this beautiful Greek island.

CHAPTER ELEVEN

MY MUST-DO LIST FOR AN UNFORGETTABLE EXPERIENCE IN KOS

To ensure your sojourn is nothing short of extraordinary, here's a curated list of 19 must-do activities that will immerse you in the heart and soul of Kos.

1. Visit the Asklepion

- **Historical Insights:** Explore the various structures of the Asklepion, including temples, stoas, and the renowned Altar of Apollo. Gain insights into ancient medical practices and the legacy of Hippocrates.
- **Scenic Views:** Enjoy panoramic views of Kos from the Asklepion's elevated position, providing a picturesque backdrop for your exploration.

2. Discover Kos Town

- **Castle of the Knights:** Roam through the Castle of the Knights, a medieval fortress that reflects the island's diverse history. The castle offers a glimpse into the strategic importance of Kos throughout the centuries.

- **Vibrant Markets:** Get lost in the vibrant markets of Kos Town. From fresh produce to local crafts, the markets showcase the island's authentic charm.

3. Relax on Paradise Beach

- **Golden Sands and Crystal Waters:** Paradise Beach is renowned for its soft golden sands and clear azure waters. Bask in the Mediterranean sun and take refreshing dips in the sea.
- **Water Activities:** Engage in water sports or simply unwind with a book on the beach. The tranquil environment makes it an ideal spot for relaxation.

4. Cycle around the Island

- **Scenic Routes:** Rent a bicycle to traverse the island's well-designed cycling paths. Discover hidden corners, olive groves, and charming villages as you pedal through the picturesque landscapes.
- **Active Exploration:** Cycling offers an active and eco-friendly way to explore Kos, allowing you to cover more ground while enjoying the island's beauty.

5. Try Local Cuisine

- **Moussaka and Souvlaki:** Delight your taste buds with classic Greek dishes. Moussaka, a layered casserole with eggplant and meat, and souvlaki, skewered and grilled meat, are must-tries.
- **Taverna Experience:** Visit local tavernas for an authentic dining experience. Enjoy not just the food but also the warm hospitality that characterizes Greek culture.

6. Take a Boat Tour

- **Island Hopping:** Embark on a boat tour to explore neighboring islands and their unique attractions. Whether it's a secluded beach or a historical site, boat tours offer diverse experiences.
- **Aegean Sea Beauty:** Revel in the beauty of the Aegean Sea, with its crystal-clear waters and the gentle sway of the boat creating a serene and memorable atmosphere.

7. Visit Ancient Agora

- **Historical Significance:** Walk among the ruins of the Ancient Agora, once a bustling marketplace and a central hub for social and economic activities in ancient times.

- **Architectural Remnants:** Marvel at the architectural remnants, including columns and statues, which provide glimpses into the island's rich history.

8. Relax in Therma Beach

- **Natural Warm Springs:** Experience the therapeutic properties of Therma Beach's warm springs. The naturally heated waters are known for their relaxing and rejuvenating effects.
- **Scenic Surroundings:** Enjoy the beach's unique setting, surrounded by rocks and cliffs, creating a secluded and tranquil atmosphere.

9. Explore Kefalos Village

- **Authentic Atmosphere:** Immerse yourself in the authenticity of Kefalos Village. The traditional architecture, narrow streets, and welcoming locals provide a genuine Greek village experience.
- **Stunning Views:** Climb to vantage points in Kefalos for breathtaking views of the coastline and the Aegean Sea, offering excellent photo opportunities.

10. Windsurf in Mastichari

- Mastichari is a windsurfer's paradise with its steady winds and azure waters. Whether you're a seasoned windsurfer or a beginner, there are schools and rental facilities available to help you ride the waves. Feel the adrenaline as you glide over the Aegean Sea, surrounded by the picturesque landscape of Kos.

11. Hike to Mount Dikaios

- For nature enthusiasts and adventure seekers, a hike to Mount Dikaios is a must. The trail takes you through scenic landscapes, offering panoramic views of the island and the Aegean Sea. The summit provides a breathtaking vantage point, especially during sunrise or sunset, creating an unforgettable hiking experience.

12. Visit the Tree of Hippocrates

- Situated in the heart of Kos Town, the Tree of Hippocrates is a living testament to the island's historical significance. Legend has it that Hippocrates, the father of medicine, taught his students under this ancient plane tree. Explore the surrounding area, which also includes the Platane Tree Square and the Archaeological Museum.

13. Sunset at Zia

- Zia, a mountain village nestled in the Dikaios range, offers one of the most spectacular sunset views on the island. As the sun sets, painting the sky with vibrant hues, enjoy the tranquil atmosphere and treat yourself to local cuisine in one of the traditional tavernas. It's a romantic and magical experience that will stay with you.

14. Day Trip to Nisyros

- Take a boat trip to the volcanic island of Nisyros, an otherworldly destination with its unique geology. Explore the village of Mandraki, built on the edge of a volcanic crater, and witness the active Stefanos crater, emitting sulfuric fumes. Nisyros provides a fascinating contrast to the serene beauty of Kos.

15. Experience Local Festivals

- If your visit coincides with a local festival, you're in for a treat. Participate in traditional celebrations, which often include music, dance, and religious processions. It's a chance to witness the vibrant culture of Kos and engage with the warmth of the local community.

16. Relax at Agios Stefanos Beach:

- Escape the crowds and unwind at Agios Stefanos Beach. Known for its calm waters and tranquil surroundings, it's an ideal spot for relaxation. Bring a book, soak up the sun, and enjoy the serenity of this hidden gem.

17. Take a Dip in Bubble Beach:

- Experience the natural wonder of Bubble Beach, where underwater vents create effervescent bubbles as you swim. It's a unique and fun activity that adds an extra element of excitement to your beach day. The phenomenon is sure to bring a smile to your face.

18. Visit Antimachia Castle:

- Explore the medieval charm of Antimachia Castle, a historic site that offers not only a glimpse into the island's past but also panoramic views of the surrounding landscapes. Walk through its ancient walls and towers, imagining the stories that unfold within its historical embrace.

19. Attend a Greek Night:

- Wrap up your Kos adventure by attending a Greek Night. These lively events often include traditional music, dance performances, and a feast of local delicacies. Engage with the warm hospitality of the locals, and immerse yourself in the joyous atmosphere of Greek festivities, creating lasting memories of your time in Kos.

By embarking on this comprehensive list, you're sure to create memories that will last a lifetime on the enchanting island of Kos.

CONCLUSION

In conclusion, embarking on a journey to Kos, Greece, promises an unforgettable experience filled with a harmonious blend of history, natural beauty, and vibrant culture. The island's charm lies in its ability to cater to diverse interests, offering something for every traveler.

From the ancient healing sanctuary of Asklepion to the bustling streets of Kos Town, visitors are treated to a sensory journey through time. The must-do list ensures a holistic exploration, whether it's cycling along picturesque paths, indulging in delectable local cuisine, or basking in the sun on the golden shores of Paradise Beach.

The island's treasures extend beyond its terrestrial borders. Boat tours beckon adventurers to uncover hidden coves, neighboring islands, and the secrets of the Aegean Sea. Whether you find yourself windsurfing in Mastichari, hiking to the summit of Mount Dikaios, or simply enjoying a serene moment at Agios Stefanos Beach, each experience contributes to the mosaic of memories that make Kos a truly special destination.

Kos doesn't just offer a feast for the eyes and the palate; it invites visitors to immerse themselves in the traditions and festivities that define its culture. Attending a Greek Night or participating in local celebrations adds a layer of authenticity to the journey, allowing travelers to connect with the heart and soul of the island.

As the sun sets over Zia and the waves gently lap the shores of Nisyros, the allure of Kos becomes evident. It's not just a travel destination; it's an invitation to discover, to explore, and to create lasting memories. The comprehensive guide ensures that every facet of this enchanting island is explored, making the journey an indelible chapter in the traveler's personal adventure book.

In the end, a visit to Kos is not just a vacation; it's an odyssey through history, a communion with nature, and a celebration of life in the heart of the Aegean. The memories forged on this island will linger, painting a vivid tapestry of a travel experience that transcends the ordinary and becomes, in every sense, unforgettable.

As you plan your trip to Kos, keep in mind that this guide is just the beginning. Kos is a dynamic and ever-changing island, with new attractions and experiences popping up all the time. So don't be afraid to explore beyond the pages of this guidebook and discover the city for yourself.

We hope this guide has provided you with the inspiration and information you need to plan an unforgettable trip to Kos. It doesn't matter if you're visiting for the first time or returning for a repeat visit, we know you will fall in love with this beautiful island and all that it has to offer.

ON A FINAL NOTE

The information provided in this travel guide is intended for general informational purposes as diligent effort has been made to ensure the accuracy of the information provided. Readers are solely responsible for their own travel decisions and activities and should use their judgment when following the suggestions and recommendations provided in this guide. Note that prices, hours of operation, and other details are subject to change without notice. It is always advisable to check with the relevant authorities, businesses, or organizations before making any travel plans or reservations.

The inclusion of any specific product, service, business, or organization in this guide does not constitute an endorsement by the author. Readers are advised to take necessary precautions and follow local laws, regulations, and customs. The author and publisher of this travel guide are not responsible for any inaccuracies or omissions, nor for any damages or losses that may result from following the information provided in this guide.

Thank you for choosing this KOS TRAVEL GUIDE, and bon voyage!

MY TRAVEL NOTES

....
....
....
....
....
....
....
....
....
....
....
....
....
....
....